WINDS OF RENEWAL

✤

TIME®
LIFE
BOOKS

This volume is one of a series that chronicles the history and culture of the Native Americans. Other books in the series include:

The Cover: Holding a rawhide shield and eagle-claw dance stick, Beau Big Crow, a young powwow dancer from Oglala, South Dakota, poses in traditional dance regalia. Indian people have gathered to dance, sing, and celebrate their heritage in growing numbers since 1934, when government restrictions against communal assemblies were lifted. Today more than 1,100 powwows are held each year all across North America.

WINDS OF RENEWAL

✛

by
THE EDITORS
of
TIME-LIFE BOOKS

ALEXANDRIA, VIRGINIA

THE AMERICAN INDIANS

SERIES EDITOR: Henry Woodhead
Administrative Editor: Loretta Y. Britten

Library of Congress Cataloging in Publication Data
Winds of renewal / by the editors of Time-Life Books.
      p.   cm. — (The American Indians; 22)
      Includes bibliographical references and index.
      ISBN 0-8094-9579-1
      1. Indians of North America—History—20th century. 2. Indians of North America—Government relations. 3. Indians of North America—Politics and government. I. Time-Life Books. II. Series.
E77.W78 1996   95-37240
305.897'073'0904—dc20   CIP

CONTENTS

1
INTO AMERICA'S MAINSTREAM

2
THE RISE OF RED POWER

3
IN PURSUIT OF SOVEREIGNTY

ESSAYS

A JOURNEY OF RECOVERY

O n August 16, 1991, the remains of 31 human beings were taken from the research vaults of the Smithsonian Institution in Washington, D.C., and presented to a delegation of 70 Sisseton-Wahpeton Sioux from North Dakota. These were the bones of their ancestors, many of which had lain in storage for more than 125 years. For the Sioux, the exchange served as a rescue mission—freeing their loved ones from long years of incarceration and returning them to the earth with dignity.

The mission was the first of its kind for the Smithsonian, the result of the Indian Graves Protection and Repatriation Act, passed into law in 1990. Since then, other tribes have claimed ancestral remains and ceremonial objects from museums, universities, and private collections throughout the United States and Europe. The remains have ranged in size from a single bone to an entire skeleton.

The practice of collecting Indian bones for scientific study dates from the early 1800s. Throughout the 19th century, scientists believed that by studying the measurements of body and head sizes of human populations, they could better explain the different behavior patterns they observed in different communities. Some in the field, however, used their findings to endorse the racist theory that non-Caucasians were inferior because of their smaller, and sup-

posedly less evolved, skulls and brains. One mid-19th-century skull collector deduced from his studies that Indians were "cruel, bloodthirsty and revengeful"—a finding not unusual given the racist attitudes of the time.

By the mid-1800s, several large museums opened in the major cities of the United States, including the Smithsonian in the nation's capital. The museums, too, wanted "specimens," as well as Indian artifacts, for their collections and displays. Graverobbers—paid perhaps $20 for a complete Indian skeleton and $5 for a skull—were often used to meet these ends.

The Native American Rights Fund of Boulder, Colorado, has estimated that as many as 600,000 Indian bones are still stored in various institutions. The Sisseton-Wahpeton Sioux believe that the Smithsonian still holds 300 of their ancestors in its collection of remains, which originally included 18,650 Native Americans.

After four days of prayer and ceremony near Washington, D. C., the Sisseton-Wahpetons took the remains back to their homeland in North Dakota for burial. For many, it was a journey of mixed emotions—sadness, anger, and pride. But it also gave tribal members renewed respect for the history and culture of their people. As one member of the delegation explained, "We see this as the beginning of a journey of recovery, not necessarily of material things, but a recovery of honor, dignity, and honesty."

A procession of Sisseton-Wahpeton tribal
members solemnly carry the remains of
their ancestors through Greenbelt Park in
the suburbs of Washington, D.C., as part
of a four-day purification ceremony. When
the remains were turned over by the Smithsonian, one tribal member recalled that
the bones were "in boxes, wrapped in paper
like they were pottery." At the park, a team
of women prepared the remains by swad-
dling them in red felt and substituting
sacred tobacco and sage for the missing
bones of incomplete skeletons.

*M*en from the color guard of the Sisseton-Wahpeton Vietnam Veterans Association maintain their vigil over the remains. The veteran at left, dressed in a traditional ribbon shirt, holds a prayer feather. Others carried sacred stones brought from their home at the Lake Traverse Reservation. The veterans ensured the sanctity of the purification ceremonies and guarded the remains for 10 days, from their reception in Washington until their burial in North Dakota.

A group of young girls carry bundles of remains, some belonging to children their own age. "It has been a hard time with my two granddaughters here," said a 71-year-old woman. "One is 12 years old and she can't accept what happened to the little children."

A man uses an eagle wing to fan the flames of the "inipi," or sweat lodge, before the purification ceremony. The inipi served the Sisseton-Wahpeton delegation as a center for meditation and prayer. Along with the inipi, the ceremonial site near Washington consisted of a firepit, a tipi where the remains were kept, and a picnic area.

*N*earing the end of the journey, the funeral cortege eases through the town of Sisseton, North Dakota, on its way to the burial grounds located at Sica Hollow, 10 miles outside of town. A van, carrying the Vietnam veterans, leads the way, followed by two vehicles bearing the remains. The procession of 60 cars extended for nearly a mile.

11

*T*he voices of the Buffalo Lake Singers fill the air on the first night after the remains arrived. "It is unexplainable the feeling I've felt bringing them home," said a man who had made the trip from Washington with bundles of remains in his pickup truck. "When we made it to the valley, I felt they got up to look out, and I just broke down. We got them home finally, the end of a long journey."

*C*arrying a buffalo skull and sage, a Vietnam veteran leads an evening procession to the tipi where the remains are kept. During the day, the bundles of bones rested on cottonwood scaffolds. "Our people 200 years ago used scaffolds for knowledge," explained Gary Holy Bull, a Sioux medicine man. "The wind helped to keep that knowledge and wisdom amongst the people. It is very important for us to put these remains on scaffolds, so that their knowledge, wisdom, and experiences that they have will be passed on to us."

A group of Sioux purify the remains in the smoke of sweet sage before the bones are returned to their tipi for the night. Two sweat lodges were also erected on the burial site for conducting purification ceremonies.

W ith the final ceremony over, young men fill in the graves of the recovered ancestors. Earlier, women and girls retrieved the remains from the scaffolds after first painting their own arms orange, a color symbolic of morning and evening, and of death. Prayers were uttered as each set of bones was lowered into the ground and returned to Mother Earth.

A Sioux elder rests in the shade of a ceremonial scaffold on a day of 90-degree heat. "The important thing on this trip is that we are a tribe," said one participant in the repatriation project. "We all belong together. The Sisseton-Wahpeton tribe is much stronger for this, and we'll be stronger in the future because of what we've done for our people."

1

Chief Bird Rattler of the Blackfeet congratulates President Franklin D. Roosevelt after adopting him into the tribe on August 5, 1934. The pipe and quilled bag (inset), similar to the ones Bird Rattler presented that day, were given to Roosevelt by other Indians in appreciation for his Indian reform programs, part of the larger New Deal.

INTO AMERICA'S MAINSTREAM

Surely the most widely publicized act of courage by a Native American in the 20th century was that of Marine Private First Class Ira H. Hayes, a Pima Indian from Bapchule, Arizona. As part of the 5th Marine Division assault force during the pivotal battle for the Japanese-held island of Iwo Jima in February 1945, Hayes was one of the first Americans to reach the summit of Mount Suribachi, the heavily fortified, 546-foot extinct volcano that dominated the island's southwestern tip. There he and five other marines raised the Stars and Stripes under intense enemy fire—a deed of bravery and triumph that was immortalized in a dramatic photograph taken by Associated Press photographer Joe Rosenthal. The image appeared on millions of war bond posters and postage stamps and eventually became a monumental sculpture—the World War II Marine Memorial near Arlington National Cemetery in Virginia.

Among Native Americans, however, Hayes was far from alone in his heroism or his patriotism. Almost 25,000 Indians, more than one-third of all able-bodied Indian males between the ages of 18 and 50, served in one capacity or another before the war was over. In some tribes, enlistment figures ran as high as 70 percent. Indians fought in every branch of the military and in every theater of operation. Many did not wait to be called up but rushed to enlist. Hearing of the draft, nine young Sioux scoffed at the idea of compulsory service. Said one, "Since when has it been necessary to conscript the Sioux as fighters?" Marveling at the high percentage of Indian volunteers, an editorial writer for *The Saturday Evening Post* declared that if all Americans were as willing to serve, "We would not need the Selective Service."

The Bureau of Indian Affairs (BIA) was never able to compile a complete reckoning of the large number of decorations the Indians won. A partial tally included no fewer than two Medals of Honor, 51 Silver Stars, 47 Bronze Stars, 71 Air Medals, and 34 Distinguished Flying Crosses. Ira Hayes, while being shuttled around a grateful America with two fellow survivors of the Iwo Jima flag raising to appear at war bond rallies, might have been the first to suggest that other stories of Indian courage, initiative, and resourcefulness rivaled or even surpassed his own.

One of the most intriguing Indian achievements was that of the Marine Corps' Navajo Code Talkers, who operated in the Pacific. Speaking a combination of their own language and newly created words for military terminology, the Indians reduced the time required for encoding and decoding radio and telephone messages by half and confounded Japanese efforts to decipher them. For security reasons, the Navajos' accomplishment was not revealed until after the war.

Indian men were not alone in their contribution to America's war effort. Native American women also served, volunteering by the hundreds for the nursing corps, the military auxiliaries, and the Red Cross. And another 40,000 Indian men and women left the reservations each year to fill personnel shortages in ordnance depots, aircraft factories, shipyards, railroads, and other war-related industries.

Shortly after the war, the Bureau of Indian Affairs published a pamphlet chronicling some of the Indians' wartime sacrifices and achievements. While lauding Indian loyalty on the home front, it featured stories of the fighting men at Bataan and Corregidor, on Iwo Jima and Okinawa, during the decisive landings at Anzio and in Normandy, and in other exotic locations that had become American household words.

Among the courageous exploits described in the pamphlet were those of Private Ben Quintana, a Keres Indian from Cochiti Pueblo in New Mexico, who before joining the army had been one of America's most promising young artists, winning first prize in a magazine contest that attracted more than 50,000 entries. While serving in the Philippines as an ammunition carrier for a machine gun squad, Quintana took part in an assault on a Japanese strong point. The Japanese suddenly counterattacked in overwhelming numbers, killing the machine gunner and severely wounding the assistant gunner. According to the citation for his posthumously awarded Silver Star, Quintana "gallantly rushed forward to the silenced gun and delivered a withering fire into the enemy, inflicting heavy casualties" before he suffered wounds that caused his death. "By this extraordinary courage he repulsed the counterattack and prevented the envelopment of the right flank of his troop," the citation recorded. His "unflinching devotion to duty and heroism under fire inspired his troop to attack and seize the enemy strong point."

Another story related the heroics of Lieutenant William R. Frederberg, a Menominee Army Air Corps pilot from Wisconsin, who won the

Private First Class Ira H. Hayes, a Pima Indian from Bapchule, Arizona, points to himself, the rearmost figure in the famous photograph of six Marines raising the American flag on Mount Suribachi, Iwo Jima. Only three of the six men in the picture survived the epic 34-day battle.

Distinguished Flying Cross, the nation's highest aviation honor, while serving with the Eighth Air Force in Europe. According to the citation, Frederberg "demonstrated superior skill in the execution of a dive bombing attack upon a heavily defended marshaling yard wherein he personally destroyed three locomotives and thereafter in the face of heavy and accurate enemy fire remained in the target area strafing installations until his ammunition was exhausted." Another Distinguished Flying Cross winner, Sergeant Shuman Shaw, a Paiute tail gunner in a B-24 Liberator, shot down two German aircraft and possibly three more on a single bombing raid—all after being badly wounded. Shaw recovered and continued to fly missions until he suffered disabling wounds in an attack against enemy installations in Budapest.

At least one Indian distinguished himself on two war fronts. Sergeant Clifford Etsitty, a 20-year-old Navajo on night patrol on the island of Attu in the Aleutians, ambushed and killed 40 Japanese soldiers during three weeks of combat in 1943. Etsitty was then wounded by a Japanese mortar. After Attu was retaken and Etsitty's wounds had healed, he was transferred to Europe where he furthered his reputation as a fighter. Once

when a patrol he was leading came under intense fire from a German machine gun nest 30 yards away, Etsitty lay prone and squeezed off exactly six rounds, killing all six of the enemy. And on another occasion, he pulled two injured comrades to safety despite the fact that he himself had been wounded by shrapnel.

In all theaters, more than 550 Indians lost their lives during the war, 30 on Iwo Jima alone, and at least another 700 were wounded. The accounts of their gallantry appealed to the sentiments of white Americans, many of whom who saw the Indian heroes as shining examples of a united democracy fighting against fascist tyranny. The tales of bravery were not unexpected. Most whites stereotyped all Indians as natural-born warriors and had always been happy to have them on their side in a fight. No less an authority than General Douglas MacArthur characterized the Indian soldier as "particularly able."

During the Civil War, Indians—mainly Cherokees, Chickasaws, Choctaws, Creeks, and Seminoles—fought for both the Union and the Confederacy. In the last of the Indian wars in the 1870s, Apaches, Crows, Sioux, and others had distinguished themselves as scouts for the U.S. Cavalry. And during World War I, more than 10,000 Indians joined the military, even though they were not eligible for the draft. Among them were

Tohono O'odham (Papago) Indians register for the selective service at the Saint Xavier Mission in Arizona on October 16, 1940. This was the first draft that included Indians, who had been granted citizenship in 1924 in recognition of their voluntary military service during World War I.

some Choctaws assigned to a signal unit of Oklahoma's 142d Infantry Regiment, who used their Muskogean dialect to communicate messages during the Meuse-Argonne campaign and became the model for the Navajo Code Talkers of World War II fame.

What made World War II different from the other wars—other than its sheer scale—was the new dimension that the vast global conflict opened to Indian life. For the first time, large numbers of tribal people who had never been beyond the boundaries of their reservations traveled far away to large cities and distant lands where they had their first real look at the outside world. Unlike African Americans who were segregated into their own units, Indian soldiers, sailors, airmen, and marines fought side by side with whites. Most of them were well received by their comrades in arms and by the military command.

The integration of Indians into white units was a conscious policy of the War Department. It happened over the objections of John Collier, President Franklin D. Roosevelt's reform-minded commissioner of Indian affairs. Collier wanted Indians to serve in all-Indian divisions in the belief that keeping them together would help preserve their tribal cultural identities. But Secretary of War Henry L. Stimson refused to form all-Indian units (a few signal corps units, including the Navajo Code Talkers were the

Howard Tiger, the first Seminole volunteer in the Marine Corps, displays his uniform to relatives at the Seminole Indian Agency in Fort Myers, Florida, in 1942. "The Indians have responded earnestly and even enthusiastically to the challenge of the war," said Indian commissioner John Collier. "From the remotest parts of isolated reservations has come evidence of Indian concern."

only exceptions). Stimson even resisted placing more than one Indian in the same platoon, because he believed that the experience of serving alone among whites would hasten the absorption of the Indian veterans into white society—an idea that ran counter to Collier's philosophy.

Indians who worked in the civilian sector experienced a similar exposure to new people and places. The war made them visible in society and brought them acceptance from many whites who had never even been face to face with an Indian before. For the first time, Indians who might have been discriminated against even on their own their home turf or limited by the paternalistic policies of the Bureau of Indian Affairs were recognized as significant figures in a collective American enterprise.

Deep wartime cuts in the budget of the Bureau of Indian Affairs also helped shape a new Indian perspective. In many ways, the prewar New Deal years under President Franklin D. Roosevelt had been the best that Native Americans had experienced in half a century. New agencies such as the Civilian Conservation Corps reached the reservations, bringing jobs, income, new schools, hospitals, and roads—making the reservation, in the words of historian Vine Deloria Jr., a Standing Rock Sioux, "less a prisoner-of-war camp and more a home." Backed by the strong advocacy of John Collier, Congress removed the ban on Indian religious ceremonies and in 1934 passed the Indian Reorganization Act, a landmark piece of legislation that stopped the erosion of tribal landholdings brought about by the allotment provisions of the Dawes Severalty Act of 1887. In addition, Collier dramatically increased the Indian presence in the Bureau of Indian Affairs, raising the number of Indians in permanent positions to more than 5,000—a nearly threefold increase.

Still, there was heated Indian opposition to much of what Collier was trying to accomplish. Not all tribes welcomed his mystical beliefs in the values of group living. Modern-minded Indians who favored assimilation into white society thought Collier's reforms were calculated to send them "back to the blanket," while many traditional tribal leaders feared losing their authority in the white-style democracy Collier proposed for every Indian community, regardless of its ancestral leadership pattern. Collier's fiercest critic, the American Indian Federation, an Oklahoma-based organization that advocated full Indian citizenship rights, argued that under Collier the BIA was promoting anti-Christian, communistic policies that only perpetuated white control of Indians and Indian lands.

A COLLECTION OF INDIAN VOICES

The revitalization of Indian pride that has taken place since World War II has been bolstered by a profusion of gifted Native American creative writers. Since the 18th century, when Indians first began writing for publication in English, they have used the power of the pen not only to explain Indian values and beliefs to white society but also as a weapon in the struggle to preserve and protect their own cultural identities. In his 1902 autobiography, the Dakota Sioux Charles Eastman explained how Sioux boys learned the oral tradition of their people by listening "with parted lips and glistening eyes" to the tales of their elders. Like those storytellers of old, modern Indian writers are also transmitters of culture, passing on their heritage to successive generations while sharing it with the wider world.

Samson Occom, a Mohegan Presbyterian minister, was the first Native American writer to be published in English. The sermon he delivered at the execution of a fellow Mohegan, who had been convicted of murder while intoxicated, came out in 1772 and was reprinted 19 times. The sermon warned of the harmful effects of alcohol on Indian life.

John Rollin Ridge (seated, far left, as part of a Cherokee delegation to Washington, D.C., in 1886) was a novelist, journalist, and poet who owned and edited several California newspapers. Ridge sometimes wrote under the name Yellow Bird, a translation of his Cherokee name Cheesquatalawny.

Mourning Dove, also known as Christine Quintasket, a Salish Indian from the state of Washington, was the first Indian woman to publish a novel in English. Her book, "Cogewea, the Half-Blood," released in 1927, describes the struggles of a mixed-blood woman to find her place in the world.

POETS, WRITERS, AND EDUCATORS

N. Scott Momaday (right), a Kiowa-Cherokee poet, novelist, and painter, shown here in 1980, raised American Indian writing to a new level of critical acclaim when his first novel, "House Made of Dawn," won the Pulitzer Prize for Literature in 1969. Momaday has taught English and comparative literature at the University of California at Berkeley and Santa Barbara, at Stanford University, and at the University of Arizona.

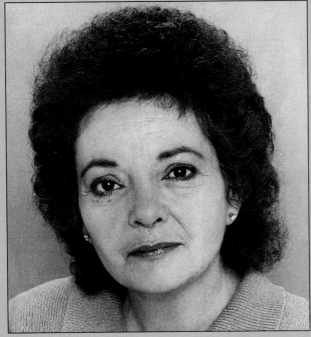

Paula Gunn Allen (left), of Laguna Pueblo, Sioux, and Lebanese descent, grew up living one of the major themes pervading her poems and novels—the spiritual search for self-identity. Through her own works and as an educator, Allen has made Native American writing accessible to broad audiences with collections like "Spider Woman's Granddaughters," or critical studies like "The Sacred Hoop: Recovering the Feminine in American Indian Traditions."

Joy Harjo (left), a Creek, has won numerous awards for poetry. Explaining her obligations as a writer, she has said, "I feel strongly that I have a responsibility to all the sources that I am: to all past and future ancestors, to my home country, to all places that I touch down on and that are myself, to all voices, all women, all of my tribe, all people, all earth, and beyond that to all beginnings and endings."

Louise Erdrich, a Turtle Mountain Ojibwa, and Michael Dorris, a Modoc (right), are award-winning writers whose stories involve characters drawn from their individual experiences. Since their marriage in 1981, most of the couple's efforts, both fiction and nonfiction, have been collaborative. Explaining their unique style of working together, Dorris has said, "We achieve consensus on every word."

PERFORMERS ON THE STAGE

In a performance of "Fires on the Water" (above), members of Alaska's Naa Kahidi Theater combine traditional costumes, music, dance, and narration—both in English and in the languages of the performers—to bring ancient stories to life. "To us," one member offered, "these stories represent the wisdom of our grandparents. They are literally the truth, and as important as anything ever written down."

Susan Aglukark (left), an Inuit singer-songwriter from Canada's Northwest Territories, sings in both English and Inuit, mixing traditional tales with sometimes dark stories of contemporary struggles. "I think music unifies cultures," she once said. "It's the one thing that everybody can sit down and get a message from."

Two Native actors, one with face covered, enact a scene from "Son of Ayash," a modern play adapted from a Cree legend and staged by the Toronto-based Native Earth Performing Arts, Inc. Formed in 1982, the theater company was designed to provide support to Indian artists and a platform for addressing the concerns of indigenous peoples, especially those in urban settings.

In 1942, as America's war machine accelerated, the Bureau of Indian Affairs headquarters was transferred to Chicago to free up valuable office space in Washington, D.C., for higher-priority wartime programs. The Indian New Deal programs faltered and gradually died out for lack of funding, making the paternalistic hand of the BIA less visible on the reservations. Indian leaders began looking more to each other rather than to the government for assistance in solving their problems.

The problems remained plentiful. Despite the jobs created by the New Deal programs, the median annual income of Indian families living on reservations in 1940 was only about $500, less than one-fourth of that earned by American white families at the time. There were exceptions. Oklahoma Indians were growing increasingly oil rich, and Oregon's Klamath were prospering as landlords of leased timberland. But most Indians were still significantly disadvantaged and as a group remained, in one scholar's words, "America's outsider, its most isolated minority."

But after the war, after earning good money while working in factory jobs, after serving with or sometimes in command of whites, after winning white respect by the application of courage and skill and the sacrifice of life and limb, after being themselves looked upon as "rich" victors in impoverished lands (and sometimes bringing home foreign-born brides), Indian expectations had risen dramatically. Second-class citizenship was no longer acceptable to them. Inspired by the legacy of the New Deal and their wartime experiences, Native Americans took a very different view of the United States and of the times in which they lived. Most important of all was the transformation in how Indians saw the possibilities for the future: A great many of them now believed they could and would have their fair share of it.

That new attitude toward their opportunities for a better life would be a strong if not always effective force in the Native American story over the ensuing decades. It would fuel legal struggles to right old wrongs. It would steel resistance against new attempts to deprive them of their rights and property. And occasionally it would explode into direct and sometimes dangerous confrontations designed to draw the attention of the American public to Indian resolution to fit tribal life into the national mosaic and determine their own destiny.

The war was nearing its end when, in mid-November 1944, citizens of

Navajo women sign a formal agreement outlawing the use of the swastika in February 1940 (above) because of its appropriation by Adolf Hitler as the symbol of Nazi Germany. The Hopi, Papago, and Apache also agreed to the ban. A common motif in many pieces of southwestern art such as this Apache basket (left), the swastika was traditionally an Indian symbol of good luck.

The war was nearing its end when, in mid-November 1944, citizens of Denver were surprised to see scores of Indians descending on the city's Cosmopolitan Hotel. Described as the largest gathering of intertribal leadership to that time, they were there to found what would become the most important Native American organization, the National Congress of American Indians, commonly called the NCAI. Nearly 80 delegates from 50 tribes, groups, and associations in 27 states attended this initial meeting. Most of them were well educated and prominent in the professions and business; eight of them were women.

Indian employees of the Bureau of Indian Affairs had laid the groundwork for the conference. The strongest promoters of the idea were D'Arcy McNickle, an anthropologist and Collier's special assistant, who although of Canadian Cree, French, and Irish ancestry, was an adopted member of the Flathead tribe in western Montana; and Mark Burns, an Ojibwa and Indian Bureau field representative in Minnesota. Other charter members included Ben Dwight, a Choctaw from Oklahoma; Archie Phinney, a Nez Percé anthropologist who was superintendent of the Northern Idaho Indian Agency; Charlie Heacock, a Sioux from the Rosebud Reservation in South Dakota; and three Cherokee women: Lois Harlan, Erma Hicks, and

Ruth Muskrat Bronson. All of them recognized that the time was ripe to capitalize on the experiences and positive images of Indians that had been generated by the war to help protect and expand Indian gains. Voicing the hopes of all the delegates, Mark Burns wrote in a private letter, "When the boys come home, we will be in a position to help them present their views to the Indian service, to state governments, or to Congress."

The concept of a pan-tribal organization was not new, of course, but earlier attempts at realizing the dream, such as the Society of American Indians, which was formed in 1911 and disbanded in 1923, had been riven by factional disputes and rendered largely ineffectual. Now, in 1944, the more politically experienced Indians recognized that only a united front could create a voice to speak for the collective interests of all Indians. Ben Dwight warned the assembled delegates of the need to achieve consensus. "I know that you can't put the same blanket over everybody because when you do that you are going to pull it off of somebody else," he said in the keynote address. "The same blanket won't go over everybody at the same time, but if you use some judgment you can spread the blanket out so that the one that is a little bit colder can get warmth from it."

Following Dwight's advice, the NCAI founders took care to make sure the assembly embraced a mix of Indian attitudes. Even though most of the founding members were themselves supporters of Collier and the Indian Reorganization Act, they recognized that Collier's opponents also had to be represented if the organization was to fulfill its broad goals—defined in the preamble to its constitution as securing "to ourselves and our descendants the rights and benefits to which we are entitled under the laws of the United States, the several states thereof, and the territory of Alaska; to enlighten the public toward a better understanding of the Indian race; to preserve Indian cultural values; to seek an equitable adjustment of tribal affairs; to secure and to preserve rights under Indian treaties with the United States; and to otherwise promote the common welfare of the American Indians."

On November 15, the meeting's first day, rumors spread that the whole enterprise was a trick to boost the Bureau of Indian Affairs and its Indian New Deal. But Ben Dwight, who had no connection with the bureau, was on hand to testify publicly that the program was free of Bureau of Indian Affairs control. The delegates took several days to hammer out an organizational framework and further define their purposes. Highest

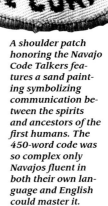

A shoulder patch honoring the Navajo Code Talkers features a sand painting symbolizing communication between the spirits and ancestors of the first humans. The 450-word code was so complex only Navajos fluent in both their own language and English could master it.

Wearing their military decorations and association shoulder patch, a group of World War II Navajo Code Talkers gather at the Special Warriors Celebration at Window Rock, Arizona, in 1991. The ceremony honored all Navajo veterans and welcomed home tribespersons who took part in Operation Desert Storm.

on the list of priorities were three subjects: protecting tribal lands, obtaining full citizenship rights, and achieving greater Indian involvement in the federal decision-making process.

Initially, some delegates wanted the NCAI constitution to forbid BIA employees from serving as NCAI officers because they were perhaps too "cosmopolitan" and not sufficiently representative of the bulk of reservation Indians. That motion was defeated, but none of the first officers were BIA people. The man elected president, Napoleon B. Johnson, was an Oklahoma Supreme Court justice and a Cherokee; the vice president, Ojibwa Edward L. Rogers, was a Minnesota lawyer; and Dan Madrano, the secretary-treasurer, was a Caddo and a member of the Oklahoma state legislature. Only two BIA employees, McNickle and Phinney, were among the people named to the NCAI's council. And the organization's rules made clear that it was not trying to impose its decisions on any tribal

council. Membership was restricted to people of Indian ancestry, either as individuals or collectively as chapters or tribes. It was also decided to admit non-Indians as nonvoting associates.

The meeting drew national attention. *Business Week* wrote that the "tribes are sounding a war cry for liberty." Perhaps the *Denver Post* was closer to the truth, if even more patronizing, in observing that the NCAI's purpose was to tell the country "that Chief Big Feather is a Good Joe," since lobbying would be the group's main function. Indians sorely needed a voice in Washington; that very year, mutterings were heard in Congress about subversive doings on the reservations. Especially from the standpoint of Native Americans who wanted to preserve their tribal identities and tribal lands, much lobbying would be needed in the postwar years. Many Americans in and out of Congress, including some Indians, believed the best hope for the future lay in removing all Native Americans from reservations and government protection and throwing them into the social and economic melting pot.

Clouding the argument was the tribes' contradictory legal standing within the United States—being at once both sovereign nations whose lands were guaranteed by treaty and wards of the federal government. Congressman Karl Mundt of South Dakota voiced the opinion of many white assimilationists when he wrote that Indians could never be accepted as full citizens so long as the Interior Department, through the Bureau of Indian Affairs, held Indian lands in trust for the tribes. "An Indian Bureau

Charter members of the National Congress of American Indians assemble for a group photograph outside the Cosmopolitan Hotel in Denver, Colorado, site of the first convention, held in November 1944. The NCAI's original president, Judge Napoleon B. Johnson, a Cherokee (front row, 10th from left), stated the organization's goal: "Indian leadership should contribute to the formulation of federal policy and should take the leading part in inquiring into the needs of the Indians and making those needs vocal."

Letha Lamb, a Pima from Sacaton, Arizona, and winner of the 1995 Miss National Congress of American Indians, wears traditional shell jewelry gathered from the shores of the Gila River and a choker with a circular design representing humankind's walk through the maze of life.

is no more necessary than a bureau to handle problems for Italians, French, Irish, Negroes, or any other racial group," Mundt declared. Other politicians saw the so-called Indian problem more in geopolitical terms. Senator George Malone of Nevada wondered aloud why the United States was "spending billions of dollars fighting communism" while at the same time maintaining tribal governments and reservations, "which are natural socialist environments." The disposition of postwar America, shaped in large part by the rising new threat posed by worldwide communism, would sorely test Ben Dwight's notion of a "shared blanket" for Indians.

Changes in his personal life and growing frustrations as commissioner caused John Collier to resign as head of the Bureau of Indian Affairs two months after the founding of the NCAI. Most of the prominent members of the NCAI had served in the armed forces or had worked in war industries at home. As *The New York*

THE YELLOWTAIL LEGACY

No sooner had the federal government set aside 38 million acres for the Crow people in 1851 than legislators and officials began to whittle the area down. Within 50 years, the reservation had been reduced to the two million acres it covers today in southeastern Montana. Like most American Indian tribes, the Crow were deprived not only of their land but also of their way of life. Authorities forced buffalo hunters to become farmers, divided communal lands, sent children off to boarding schools that suppressed the Crow language and culture, and banned the Sun Dance, central to the tribe's spiritual life.

In the 20th century, two brothers raised on the reservation took a stand for their people. Robert Yellowtail, a lawyer, entered politics to preserve what remained of the tribe's territory and autonomy. Thomas Yellowtail, a medicine man, worked with the Crow and other groups to revive ancestral beliefs and practices, including the Sun Dance. Defending Crow interests became a family tradition, carried on politically in recent years by Robert's son William.

Standing high above the broad Bighorn Canyon on the Crow Reservation, a member of the tribe offers up his prayers. The father of Robert and Thomas Yellowtail, Hawk with the Yellow Tail Feathers—known simply as Yellowtail—settled on the reservation in the late 1800s. His grandson William has represented the Crow in the state legislature.

YELLOWTAIL

THOMAS YELLOWTAIL

ROBERT YELLOWTAIL

WILLIAM YELLOWTAIL

Times wrote, a "new veteran-led sense of power is everywhere in the Indian country." These young men and women wanted assurance of their right to vote (still withheld in Arizona and New Mexico) and to drink alcohol just like other adult Americans. They demanded decent educations for their children. And they hoped to continue enjoying the kinds of incomes they had had during the war, which by 1944 reached an average two-and-a-half times as high as in 1938, giving many Native Americans their first experience of a living standard that began to approach that of white Americans. They also sought redress of grievances against a government that had been violating its treaties with them and taking their lands for more than 150 years.

Since before the Civil War, Indian tribes had been denied the legal standing that would have empowered them to take the government to court over such claims without first securing authorization from Congress in the form of a special act for each individual case. Finally, in 1946, partly in response to the NCAI's persistent demands, Congress passed a law creating an Indian Claims Commission, which was to settle, decisively, all tribal grievances against the United States.

NCAI president Napoleon B. Johnson called the legislation the "most important, equitable, and constructive Indian law ever passed by Congress." Johnson, D'Arcy McNickle, and other eminent founders of the NCAI attended the ceremony held at the White House when President Harry S. Truman signed the bill into law.

The act established a special court to hear class-action suits filed by and on behalf of Native Americans to correct inadequate compensation for lands that were taken from them during the 19th century. According to the original plan, this was to have been accomplished within a five-year period. But by the end of the five years, petitioners had swamped the commission with more than 800 cases, including claims for denial of treaty-recognized hunting and fishing rights and transgressions against water and mineral rights as well as for illegal seizures of land.

It was clear that considerable time would be required to deal with all the cases. The problem was made worse by the Justice Department's laboriously picking through every ancient record with a fine-tooth comb to tot up even small government expenditures on a tribe's behalf—for blankets, plows, and cookware, for example—which would be deducted from the final settlement. Moreover, land was paid for according to its value when taken from the Indians, a fraction of its modern worth. In some cases, the award valuation was too low even by historical standards. California

Volunteers in Los Angeles, California, load food, clothing, and medical supplies for shipment to impoverished Navajos living near Gallup, New Mexico, in the winter of 1947. The economic crisis, precipitated by the return to the reservation of some 3,600 Navajo war veterans, was exacerbated by bitterly cold weather and severe snowstorms.

tribes, for instance, got only forty-seven cents an acre for their land, much less than they could have obtained had they sold it on the open market during the 19th century, to say nothing of the asking price in 1950.

Although in time the commission awarded approximately two billion dollars to the tribes, deductions for government expenses, including Indian legal fees, reduced the total available to the Indians to about $800 million. Still, while lower than it should have been, this sum proved to be a major impetus for Indian economic development, helping underwrite tribal business enterprises, reservation development, and the construction of Indian community centers, as well as funding scholarships to allow Indian youth to gain access to education and technical skills. The commission's charter was repeatedly renewed until 1978, when Congress finally allowed it to lapse. All leftover cases have subsequently been transferred to the U.S. Court of Claims.

Meanwhile, Native Americans secured relief on some other fronts. In 1948 federal and state courts overturned laws that kept Indians from voting in Arizona and New Mexico. And in 1953, Congress finally made it legal for Native Americans to buy firearms and purchase alcohol off the reservations on the same basis as other citizens. Both issues had been particular sore spots for the Indian veterans. The question of whether to end or maintain prohibition on a reservation was left up to each tribe.

Native American hopes of maintaining their wartime prosperity, however, dwindled quickly, as defense industries shut down, throwing many out of work. Returning veterans soon learned that jobs were either scarce or nonexistent. "We are forgotten men in a land of plenty," declared Robert Yellowtail, a Crow Indian leader disillusioned with the slow rate of Indian progress in 1948. "We are prisoners in the land of our birth."

Early in the postwar years, two new issues arose between Native Americans and the United States government—federal programs that were known by the ominous names *relocation* and *termination,* terms chillingly redolent of the recent war's totalitarian vocabularies. Both policies were aimed at removing Native Americans from their federally protected reservations and integrating them into the national economy. In the eyes of many Indians and a substantial number of whites, the ultimate goal, especially in the case of termination, was not only to relieve the government of its "Indian burden" but—as in other previous efforts—to relieve the Indians of their land.

Relocation, which offered training and support for Native Americans who wanted to leave the reservation and take work in a city, actually had beneficial effects. No one was compelled to relocate, and those who found jobs and succeeded in adjusting to urban life generally enjoyed

Navajos march from Tuba City, Arizona, to Flagstaff to protest their forced relocation as a result of the Hopi-Navajo Land Settlement Act of 1974, which attempted to establish permanent boundaries between the tribes—a measure resisted by some members of both communities. The upside-down flags are Indian symbols of protest.

An Ojibwa family watches television in their comfortable Oakland, California, home in 1955. Such photographs portraying the white ideal of assimilation hid the fact that many Indians who left their homelands for the cities experienced a deep sense of cultural loss.

greater incomes than those who stayed home on the reservations. In the early 1950s, the BIA opened field relocation offices in eight American cities from Cleveland to Los Angeles. Later, the bureau set up special vocational education centers near cities and near reservations. The BIA provided training, transportation, job-placement assistance, and some subsistence money to help new urban workers get started. In 1952 the bureau spent half a million dollars on the program; by 1965 it was spending $11.5 million a year. Congress was willing to provide funding because it foresaw future rewards from relocation. "The sooner we can get the Indians into cities," declared Senator Arthur Watkins of Utah, chairman of the Senate Select Committee on Indian Affairs, "the sooner the government can get out of the Indian business."

By the middle of the 1970s, the government relocation program had helped 160,000 Indians take up urban existence. Nevertheless, some 75 percent of the Native Americans who moved into cities did so on their own, with no special training or federal aid, motivated in most cases solely by the desire to achieve a higher standard of living. Many of them were veterans or Indians who had worked off the reservation during the war. Others were simply searching for a better life. The number of Indians in urban areas more than doubled every decade from 1950 until 1980, and by that latter year, city dwellers for the first time made up more than half of the Native American population. In 1990 the figure had reached more than 1.4 million—78 percent.

The statistics say nothing of all the personal pathos and adjustment involved in such a sweeping change. Pain has been part of it. Marine hero Ira Hayes, who helped raised the flag on Iwo Jima but never felt comfortable with the fame thrust upon him, was relocated to Chicago in 1953 and before long drank his way to skid row. Later, while Hayes was living in Los Angeles and then Arizona, he was frequently arrested for public intoxication and in 1955, at the age of 33, died of exposure while drunk. Unfortunately, his story—widely publicized in a 1961 Hollywood film *The Outsider,* starring Tony Curtis as Hayes—was not that unusual. Even sober Native Americans were sometimes confused by the white way of life, especially its business practices. A young Navajo woman was so shocked by her employer's "blatantly immoral" custom of charging more for merchandise than he paid for it that she asked for a day off so she could report him. And almost all relocated Indians were homesick. "Even in cases where the older members of their families have passed away, they still make a point to go home" said Ben Bearskin, a Winnebago relocated to Chicago. "Many of them make the trip twice a year to go back to the place where they were born and raised."

A Cherokee named Watt Spade underscored the same point with a story he heard from two Indians in a Chicago bus station: "They said the government wanted to put a man on the moon and it could be done alright, but nobody knew how to get the guy home again after he landed on the moon. These guys said all the government had to do was put an Indian in that rocket ship and tell him he was being relocated and then, after he got to the moon, that Indian would find his own way home again, and the government wouldn't have to figure that part out at all."

Termination was the much more brutal partner of relocation. To terminate a tribe meant to end its special relationship with the federal government—to remove the government's protective shield that was guaranteed for "as long as the grass shall grow and the waters flow" in almost all treaties with Indians; to cut off the subsidies that provided the tribe's

PRESERVING A TRIBAL HERITAGE

George Hunt, born in 1854 to a white father and an Indian mother and raised among the Kwakiutl in British Columbia, lived at a time when the native traditions of the Northwest Coast were under siege. In 1888 Hunt met anthropologist Franz Boas, who had come to the area to study Kwakiutl culture. Trained by Boas as his research assistant, Hunt collected and documented thousands of objects, including dance masks and ceremonial bowls used in potlatches and other feasts. By the time of his death in 1933, George Hunt had emerged as an authority in his own right. For Hunt and his descendants, studying the ancient customs was a way of perpetuating a culture that many thought would soon disappear. In fact, some of the dances and ceremonies Hunt documented are being performed by native people today.

An eagle on its nest crowns this wooden Kwakiutl mask collected by George Hunt in 1899. The mask was used for a dance during the dramatic winter ceremonies, when religious societies initiated new members.

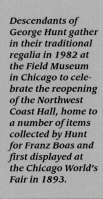

Descendants of George Hunt gather in their traditional regalia in 1982 at the Field Museum in Chicago to celebrate the reopening of the Northwest Coast Hall, home to a number of items collected by Hunt for Franz Boas and first displayed at the Chicago World's Fair in 1893.

George Hunt, holding a deerskin drum, sits with his Kwakiutl wife, Francine, in a photograph taken in 1930 in his hometown of Fort Rupert, British Columbia. Hunt's family ties to the Kwakiutl gave him access to treasures and secrets that were seldom revealed to outsiders.

Franz Boas, far left, and George Hunt hold a backdrop for a photographer taking a picture of a Kwakiutl woman spinning strands of cedar bark. Hunt himself took photographs of Kwakiutl customs to document the culture.

Richard Hunt, great-grandson of George Hunt, displays traditional Kwakiutl dance regalia to a group of school children in Victoria, British Columbia. Spread across his lap is a dance cape that he has worn during modern-day Kwakiutl winter ceremonies.

A six-foot-tall cedar totem pole topped by an eagle (left) and a raven headdress (right) are among the works carved by Richard Hunt, who mastered the craft like his father and grandfather before him. Hunt limits his carving to family and Kwakiutl symbols.

education and healthcare, dole out whatever money and property deeds were held in trust for it, end the tax-free status of the reservation, and push the tribe away from its lifeline, leaving it to sink or swim or be chewed up by rapacious loggers, miners, farmers, ranchers, or state and local governments. In the process, especially if its land base vanished, the tribal entity would become impotent and meaningless, and individual Indians supposedly would become real Americans, integrated with the rest of the country. Of course, this was not really a new idea. In purposes and method, it closely echoed the Dawes Act of 1887 that John Collier and the Indian Reorganization Act had successfully vanquished in the 1930s.

But by the 1950s, many members of Congress were eager to undo Franklin Roosevelt's reform heritage. The task force on Indian affairs of the U.S. Commission on Organization of the Executive Branch of Government, popularly known as the Hoover Commission, created by Congress in July 1947, rang the warning bell. "Assimilation must be the dominant goal of public policy," it declared. "On this point there can be no doubt." The commission's top priority was the complete integration of the Indians "into the mass of the population as full, tax-paying citizens." In large measure, the task force's recommendation was the result of the wide-

Navajos at a meeting in Cactus Valley, Arizona, in October 1981 express shock and grief upon receiving the news that they will have to give occupancy rights of their land to the neighboring Hopi Indians because of a 19th-century treaty. "In our tongue," one Navajo complained, "there is no word for relocation. To move away means to disappear and never be seen again."

Seated inside her hogan, Katherine A. Smith, a Navajo from Big Mountain, Arizona, displays the message that she has sewn onto an American flag to voice her protest against the forced relocation of her people.

spread malnutrition and starvation that plagued many Indian people after their men came home from the war, especially the Navajo during the winter of 1947-1948—a time when Americans as a whole were enjoying unprecedented prosperity and virtually full employment.

By 1952 both major political parties had pledged to "free" Indians and make them first-class citizens by removing them from their special relationship with the government. During the summer of 1953, the House and the Senate each approved without a single nay vote a concurrent resolution to "terminate" all federal responsibility to Native Americans as soon as possible. Utah's Senator Watkins referred to the action as the "Indian freedom program." Commissioner of Indian Affairs Dillon S. Myer prudently warned the Bureau of Indian Affairs staff that some tribes might not be disposed to cooperate with termination, but in spite of their objections, he said, "we must proceed."

Watkins assumed the role of gatekeeper in the termination process. Working from a list of tribes thought to be ready for the treatment, he proposed to each in turn that now was the time to ready legislation that, after a transition period of several years, would set it free. Sometimes, apparently, he did not bother telling a tribe what he was arranging. It has been alleged that he told some small groups of Paiutes in his home state of Utah that the legislation he was preparing was solely for the purpose of making their marriages legal in Utah's courts. When they assented to that, he wrote a bill that removed them from the federal government's guardianship and made them wards of a Utah bank instead.

Besides deceit, he employed threats, telling reluctant tribes that he would make sure they would never get their own money, held in trust for them by the government, unless they approved termination. A particularly egregious example of this technique and its results was Watkins's treatment of Wisconsin's Menominee. In the early 1950s, this tribe, smoothly managed by its own members, enjoyed moderate prosperity. Menominee lumbermen felled trees in the tribe's forest, and Menominee mill workers processed them at the tribe's sawmill. They were one of only three tribes to pay their own administrative costs. The tribe paid for part of its own healthcare at a nearby private hospital and most of its welfare costs.

In the settlement of a 1951 forestry dispute, the Menominee were awarded an $8-million judgment against the United States. The money, however, was ordered paid into the U.S. Treasury to be dispensed only with congressional approval. In 1953 the tribe asked for $5 million of it to be distributed at a rate of $1,500 per tribesperson. Watkins arranged for an amendment to the bill authorizing the distribution of funds: They first had to agree to termination. "'Termination!' What did *that* mean?" a spokesperson for an anti-termination group later wrote. "None of us Menominee realized what it meant!" After yielding to Watkins's demands, they learned all too soon what it meant.

Their tribe was converted into a corporation called Menominee Enterprises, Inc., or MEI. Of its nine-man board of directors, only four were from the tribe; five were outsiders. Their reservation became a county, and title to reservation land reverted to the corporation. Members of the tribe, who before had owned all land together and had never paid taxes, now had to come up with large sums to buy the land beneath their own homes and, moreover, pay taxes on it. Even so, the county did not have a sufficient tax base for public services, so MEI sold ancestral Indian land, prime lakefront plots for summer vacation houses, to non-Indians. Being operated strictly for profit now, the sawmill acquired new equipment so that the work force could be cut. Some of these newly unemployed did yard work and other chores for the white summer vacationers; others went on welfare, which the county could not afford to provide. And in a

A Lumbee Indian hits a Klansman with the butt of his rifle while another grabs the microphone that the Ku Klux Klan had rigged for an anti-Indian rally in a field near Maxton, North Carolina, on the night of January 18, 1958. The Lumbees broke up the rally without causing any serious injuries.

vindictively hurtful act, the Menominee tribal rolls were closed. "Our children born since 1954 have been legally deprived of their birthright as Menominee Indians," mourned a member.

Other Indian groups, including the Catawba, some Utes, the Klamath, the Grande Ronde, various California tribes, and the Siletz were also pushed through the termination mill. But reaction against the policy was building. The Daughters of the American Revolution used their considerable political muscle to rescue Seminoles living on their reservations in Florida from the termination that would have set them adrift in the modern world. Montana Senator Mike Mansfield saved his state's Flathead Indians with a reminder to the legislation-writing subcommittee that the tribe had been regarded as an equal when the treaty with the United States was made, and that the federal government would be shamed by breaking it. (Actually, many of the old treaties were supposedly agreed between equals, but violating them had not deterred Senator Watkins and his colleagues before this. In fact, in their push for termination, they were willing to break even the United States's oldest treaty of all, the Pickering Treaty signed by George Washington with the Seneca in 1794.)

At an emergency meeting in Washington, D.C., in 1954, the National Congress of American Indians demanded that tribes should be terminated only by their own request. The following year, three tribes—the Ottawa, Wyandot, and Peoria—did request termination, and the NCAI made a point of raising no protest. In 1958 a new secretary of the interior, Fred A. Seaton, publicly embraced the NCAI's viewpoint, stating that no tribe should be terminated against its will. Nonetheless, compulsory terminations continued, often with the assistance of the Bureau of Indian Affairs. Between 1948 and 1957, Indians lost 3.3 million acres of land that were removed from trust and sold because of termination. President Richard M. Nixon finally put an end to the policy in 1970. And in 1973 a repentant Congress restored the old status of the Menominee. Many Native Americans are not at all sure that they have seen the last of termination, however. When the American Farm Bureau Federation, a nationwide support organization for family farms, called for a resumption of termination, Elmer Savilla, director of the National Tribal Chairmen's Association, asked its leaders why. "They told me frankly that the Indians are getting too much land and water back," he said.

"Termination is here to stay," said Robert Burnette, a Rosebud Sioux and former director of the NCAI and commissioner of Indian affairs. "It is going to hit us in the face almost every day. We had better be prepared for it."

Other dangers besides termination threatened Native Americans during the late 1950s, and Indians were demonstrating an increased willingness to stand up for their rights. In January 1958, the Ku Klux Klan came looking for trouble in Robeson County, North Carolina. Robeson County was home to 40,000 whites, 30,000 Lumbee Indians, and 25,000 African Americans. The county's inhabitants basically enjoyed a peaceful existence, albeit one that had them segregated three ways, living in three separate communities, and their children sorted by race into three different school systems.

But word got around that an Indian family had moved into a white neighborhood and that an Indian girl was dating a white man, or so it was said. Apparently to frighten Indians, the Klan scheduled a nighttime rally allegedly organized by the self-styled grand wizard from South Carolina. It also attracted some 300 to 350 local Lumbees, many of them armed with rifles or shotguns. As the 75 Klansmen present grew increasingly tense, nervously eyeing the large number of Indians assembling around them, one Lumbee shot out the lone light bulb that dangled over the meeting place. Then the Lumbees charged, whooping and firing into the air. The

George Gillette, chairman of the business council of the Three Affiliated Tribes (Mandan, Arikara, and Hidatsa) on the Fort Berthold Indian Reservation in North Dakota, covers his face to hide his tears as Secretary of the Interior J. A. Krug signs a contract ceding 155,000 acres of reservation land to the government for construction of the Garrison Dam on the Missouri River in 1948. Gillette said of the deal: "The members of the tribal council sign this contract with heavy hearts."

Klansmen dropped their own weapons and fled, while the Indians shot at the tires of their cars. Because violence had been feared, there was press on hand to witness the rout, which was amply covered in national publications. No one was killed or seriously injured. Two Klansmen, including the grand wizard, were sentenced to jail for inciting to riot. It was a signal victory, one that infused with pride not only the Lumbee but numerous other Native Americans throughout the land.

Unfortunately for the Indians, in most cases victory was not so readily secured. Native Americans still found themselves up against federal bureaucracies that were perfectly willing to steamroller Indian rights. In no area was this unresponsive attitude made more clear than in disputes regarding the construction of huge dams to satisfy the growing public need for electrical power—disputes that the Indians almost always lost.

Probably no groups sustained more damage from public projects than tribes in the upper Missouri River Basin, whose lands were subjected to a vast complex of dams and reservoirs known as the Pick-Sloan Plan. Sioux historian Vine Deloria Jr. has declared that Pick-Sloan was "without doubt, the single most destructive act ever perpetrated on any tribe by the United States." Pick-Sloan, a collaborative undertaking by the Army Corps of Engineers and the Bureau of Reclamation, was estimated to cost $1.75 billion when begun in 1944. In 1970, four years after the project was completed, its total costs were calculated at $28 billion. But its real cost was paid not

Peabody Western Coal Company's strip mining operations bring both revenue and devastation to Navajo lands atop Black Mesa in Arizona. To survive after termination and government funding cuts, several western tribes, including the Navajo, have negotiated with large energy companies to strip-mine their coal, a process that removes successive layers of earth to uncover the mineral deposits beneath (right). Once the minerals are extracted, only barren pits remain (above). While many Navajos favored the economic benefits, others feared the long-term damage that the strip mining inflicts on the land.

by the government but by the Mandan, Arikara, Ojibwa, and Hidatsa of North Dakota; Montana's Cree, Crow, Blackfeet, and Assiniboin; the Shoshone and Arapaho of Wyoming; and not least, the Sioux of North and South Dakota, who saw more than 202,000 prime acres of their land disappear under the spreading waters of the Missouri River.

On paper, the Sioux loss does not appear as devastating as it actually was, since only six percent of the total area of five Sioux reservations was inundated. But the flooded land was prized, shaded bottom lands along the rivers and streams, where there was plenty of grass for livestock, firewood, game, water, and an abundance of herbs, berries, and other edibles used by the Indians not only for food but also for ceremonial and medicinal purposes. More than one-third of the Sioux living in these desirable areas were compelled to abandon their homes. The uplands where they had to relocate offered little in the way of wild food, or wood or water, and no natural protection against the broiling summer sun or bitter winter winds. Deloria, whose family has lived in the region for generations, has noted that the gigantic dams flooded not only "ancestral farms and ranches," but "memories, leaving the tribes materially and spiritually impoverished."

Indeed, in at least one instance, it seemed to the Indians that the Corps of Engineers was actually hastening the end of the world. Lone Man, the spiritual prophet-hero of North Dakota's Mandan people, long ago told them they would know the world was about to end when the Missouri River reversed its course and trees grew upside down. His words acquired new relevance in the 1950s, when the Garrison Dam stopped the river's flow and huge cottonwoods, torn form the earth by bulldozers, floated with their roots in the air.

Such wrenching upheaval also befell tribes in the East. When New York's State Power Authority (SPA) wanted to flood more than 1,200 acres of the Tuscarora Reservation to create a reservoir for a Niagara Falls hydroelectric project, the small tribe (about 650 people) actually did not think they would lose. After all, their land had been protected since 1794 by a federal government treaty guarantee. The Tuscarora had hired good lawyers. But the SPA and its chairman, Robert Moses, were not to be deterred. When the tribe turned away the surveyors, Moses sent out an open letter saying the Indians were obstructing progress.

On April 17, 1958, the tribe was waiting when the surveyors came back with an armed escort. "There were about 35 Niagara County deputy sheriffs, 50 state troopers, and a large number of plainclothesmen," recalled Tuscarora chief Richard Clinton. "In addition to the regular sidearms, these police invaders had riot equipment, tear gas, and submachine guns in their cars. With this show of force, they attempted to intimidate our people." But, wrote Clinton, "our people—men, women, and children—stood firm." Police grabbed four Indians and arrested them. Their cases were later dismissed. Surveying and other work progressed, but harassment of the tribe continued. Indians complained that their phones were tapped. In 1960 the struggle went to the U.S. Supreme Court where it was decided in favor of the New York State Power Authority by a four-to-three split decision.

"Some things are worth more than money and the costs of a new enterprise," Justice Hugo Black wrote in a dissenting opinion. "I regret that this Court is to be the governmental agency that breaks faith with this dependent people. Great nations, like great men, should keep their word.

Indians all across America agreed. Not long after the Supreme Court's final ruling, a new generation of Indian activists began laying plans to end white exploitation and prove once and for all that despite past and present injustices, the Indian peoples and their cultures had survived and were here to stay—as permanent features of modern American life. ❖

A young Navajo shepherd and a lone member of his flock cross a field adjoining the Four Corners Power Plant located in Fruitland, New Mexico. Reservation residents claim pollution from the coal-burning plant has done serious harm to their land and livestock and contaminated their water supply.

THE QUEST TO RECLAIM LOST SACRED DOMAINS

From time immemorial, Native Americans have found the Great Spirit in nature. Remote mountaintops, unusual rock formations, life-giving springs, hidden caves, and other often spectacular vistas are the cathedrals of American Indian religions. Whereas non-Indians often see such landscapes merely as examples of unspoiled natural beauty, to the Indian they are holy places, places that mark the work of spiritual figures and reflect the blessings the Creator has bestowed on the earth. Here people gather healing plants, pray, fast, seek guardian spirits, or train to be a tribal healer. As a Taos Pueblo spiritual leader said of his people's sacred Blue Lake situated high in the Sangre de Cristo Mountains: "The lake is our church. The evergreen trees are our living saints. Blue Lake is the heart of our religion."

When tribes retreated to reservations, however, many holy places became public or private land outside of tribal control. Today Indians are fighting to regain access to these areas, many of which are threatened by non-Indian interests eager to exploit them for a variety of purposes, including mining, logging, and recreation.

The American Indian Religious Freedom Act of 1978—designed by Congress to "protect and preserve the inherent right of American Indians to believe, express, and exercise their traditional religions, including access to sites"—was expected by many Indians to be a safeguard against such exploitation. But the bill lacked sufficient legal strength to guarantee these ideals, and Indian groups are working today to amend it.

Believing that the future of their sacred belief system is at stake, Native Americans argue that development diminishes, even destroys, a site's medicine power. "Every society needs sacred places," said Sioux author and attorney Vine Deloria Jr. "A society that cannot remember its past and honor it is in peril of losing its soul."

In August l971, residents of Taos Pueblo hold a ceremony called Honoring the Creator to celebrate the return of their sacred Blue Lake and surrounding lands, which were taken from them in l906. The victory marked the first time the U.S. Congress returned land to an Indian group for religious purposes. The Taos people believe that Blue Lake is the resting place for their souls and the home of supernatural beings known as the cloud people.

SANGRE DE CRISTO MOUNTAINS, NEW MEXICO

Formerly part of Carson National Forest, these 48,000 acres of the original 50,000-acre tract in the Sangre de Cristo Mountains reverted to Indian ownership in 1970. Every year kiva religious societies from Taos Pueblo make a pilgrimage 20 miles on foot or horseback to the sacred Blue Lake, some 12,000 feet above sea level. In the inset, the Rio Pueblo tumbles down the mountainside, bringing water from Blue Lake to the people of the pueblo. Today they lobby for the return of almost 800 acres along their sacred pilgrimage way that are currently being used by non-Indian hikers.

BEAR BUTTE, SOUTH DAKOTA

Rising from a sea of grass, Bear Butte is sacred to both the Chey-enne and the Lakota. A Lakota elder has described the 1,200-foot promontory as a "spiritual power dream place." Lakota owner-ship of Bear Butte was recognized in the Fort Laramie treaty of 1868, along with the rest of the Black Hills. But it was seized by the United States in 1877 and is today a state park, with roads, walkways, parking lots, viewing platforms, and a visitors' center that annually draws 100,000 tourists, who often disrupt the Indi-ans' vision quests. The Lakota have refused a cash settlement for the land, and the bitter ownership dispute remains unresolved.

MOUNT GRAHAM, ARIZONA

*Mount Graham overlooks a field of cactus plants and poppies in
the Coronado National Forest near the San Carlos Reservation in
Arizona. The Apache revere the mountain as the home of the
"gaan," or mountain spirits, who gave the tribe sacred songs and
dances and safeguard its spiritual and physical well-being. The
10,720-foot peak is the proposed site of an international observa-
tory of seven large telescopes, two of which have already been
built. In 1995 the Apache Survival Coalition succeeded in halting
further construction, pending cultural and environmental studies.*

HAVASU CANYON, ARIZONA

The Havasupai Indians have always believed that their homeland, Havasu Canyon (in Grand Canyon), and the spring that feeds their canyon's creek and falls (inset) possess healing powers. When Grand Canyon National Park was established in 1919, the federal government pressured the Indians to abandon much of their plateau lands and remain on the canyon floor. Havasupai leaders argued their case before Congress and in 1975 received 185,000 acres of highlands, the largest acreage yet returned to any tribe.

MEDICINE WHEEL, WYOMING

The ancient stone circle with 28 spokes atop Medicine Mountain has long been a ceremonial and vision quest site for Crow, Cheyenne, and other Plains Indians. In 1962 the area was designated a national historic landmark, and in time the U.S. Forest Service planned to build an access road, parking lot, and observation deck—intrusions the Indians feared would desecrate their holy spot. To the relief of the Indians, the plans were abandoned in 1991, and since then a management and protection program has enabled the various tribes to carry out their ceremonies undisturbed. Indian pilgrims visiting Medicine Wheel often leave prayer flags (inset) tied to the wire fence that surrounds the site.

MOUNT SHASTA, CALIFORNIA

This 14,000-foot-high mountain in the Cascade Range is sacred to several California tribes. The Wintu orient their burial sites toward the mountain, where they believe spirits go on their journey to the land of the dead. Pit River Indians tell of a spirit dwelling within the mountain that maintains the earth in balance with the rest of the universe. The Shasta and other tribes use the mountain for spiritual training, healing, and the gathering of medicinal plants. Today the mountain's spiritual power is jeopardized by proposals to build a ski resort and establish a logging business on its slopes.

2

THE RISE OF RED POWER

Braving the chill waters of the Bighorn River, a man fishes on Montana's Crow Reservation, which lies beyond the boundary marker in the foreground. In the 1980s, the Crow lost traditional fishing rights that had given them exclusive use of reservation waters.

It was August 10, 1961, and the streets of Gallup, New Mexico, were thronged with people attending the city's annual intertribal festival. But inside Gallup's Indian community center, 10 young college-educated Indian men and women from nine different tribes were deep in conversation. They sat cross-legged in a circle discussing ways to promote the lot of Indians everywhere. Their voices reflected a growing impatience. Two months before, several of the group had traveled to Chicago for a conference sponsored by the National Congress of American Indians, the organization founded in 1944 by tribal leaders and Indian employees of the Bureau of Indian Affairs to lobby for Indian rights. The young Indians had come away frustrated at what they perceived as the timidity of their elders.

"We saw the 'Uncle Tomahawks' fumbling around, passing resolutions, and putting headdresses on people," said Mel Thom, a Northern Paiute from Nevada and a civil engineering student at Brigham Young University. "But as for taking a strong stand, they just weren't doing it." Thom may have inherited his assertiveness—one of his ancestors was the prophet Wovoka, founder of the late-19th-century Ghost Dance religion that called for all Indians to purge themselves of the white man's ways and live together in harmony.

That day at Gallup, Thom and his colleagues decided to form a new organization called the National Indian Youth Council (NIYC). Its founding signaled the emergence of a brash new generation of Indian leaders. In the past, in their struggle to gain more control over their own affairs, Indians had generally avoided open conflict with the larger society. The new NIYC was determined to change all that. It was time, Mel Thom declared, for Indians "to raise some hell."

The Youth Council began by publishing a newspaper called *ABC: Americans Before Columbus*. Angry articles denounced older Indian leaders as "apples" because they were "red" on the outside but "white" inside. Thom and his colleagues were influenced by their African American contemporaries in the civil rights movement. Tactics of civil disobedience such as sit-ins at white-only lunch counters in the South dramatized racial discrimination by bringing mass arrests and national media attention. But the Youth Council also took a cue from recent actions by fellow Indians. By lying down in front of trucks and bulldozers, the Tuscarora in the 1950s had blocked the construction of a reservoir that would have destroyed one-fifth of their reservation in western New York. And in 1958, Lumbees in North Carolina had broken up a Ku Klux Klan rally in the Indians' home county of Robeson.

There was certainly no shortage of issues where confrontation might prove useful. Indian unemployment was 10 times higher than the national average; infant mortality stood at twice the national rate; and the average Indian life span was only 40 years. But unlike blacks who sought equal treatment under the law, the NIYC wanted Indians to be treated differently. After all, a special relationship between the tribes and the federal government had been spelled out many decades before in more than 400 treaties and agreements that bestowed certain rights and benefits upon Indians in exchange for their lands. Many Indians were demanding that the United States adhere to the old treaties so that they could remain apart—geographically, politically, and culturally. In New York, the Seneca fought in vain to prevent flooding of their valleys by the federally funded Kinzua Dam, built in violation of one of the oldest existing American treaties with Indians. In New Mexico, the Taos Pueblo Indians had been seeking the return of their sacred Blue Lake for more than a half-century. So many such issues were simmering that Robert K. Thomas, a Cherokee anthropologist and mentor to the NIYC activists, described the Indian situation as "one big seething cauldron about to explode."

The struggle that would provide the Youth Council with, in Thom's words, a "target area for direct action," occurred in Washington State. The Puyallup, Muckleshoot, and Nisqually tribes—none of them numbering more than a few hundred members—faced revocation of their century-old fishing rights along the rivers and streams flowing into Puget Sound. In 1854, in the Treaty of Medicine Creek, these and other small Indian communities living on Puget Sound had agreed to give up most of their ancestral valleys and move to reservations. Because their livelihood centered on fish, especially salmon, they insisted on a provision guaranteeing the "right of taking fish at all usual and accustomed grounds." Subsequent treaties with other tribes contained the same guarantee.

Once so plentiful an early white settler declared that he could walk across the stream on their backs, the stock of salmon and steelhead trout had been greatly reduced by pollution and the pressure of modern commercial fishing. To protect the fish swimming upriver during spawning season, the state of Washington imposed regulations limiting the fishing season and barred certain fishing methods, such as the use of gill nets. Insisting on their treaty rights, Indians defied these conservation laws. When game wardens began attacking the Indian fishermen with billy clubs and the Indians struggled, they were charged with resisting arrest. Indians all across the country saw these arrests as just another example of whites once again depriving a few hundred Native Americans of the source and symbol of their physical and spiritual sustenance.

From the beginning of the 20th century, almost all the court tests of the applicability of state fishing laws to Indians in the state of Washington and elsewhere supported the Indians' claims to special rights. Yet in late 1963, the Supreme Court of the state of Washington ruled that the state did have the right to regulate Indian fishing for purposes of conservation. The judgment, in effect, nullified the old Medicine Creek treaty.

The Puget Sound tribes decided they were too small and fragmented to wage the struggle alone and invited representatives of the National Indian Youth Council to help organize their protest. Working closely with a newly formed local group, the Survival of American Indians Association, the NIYC brought together representatives from some 40 tribes to plan a campaign. At last the organization had a testing ground. Copying the lunch-counter sit-ins in the South, the Indians would lead "fish-ins."

The fish-ins began in earnest in February 1964 when the steelhead trout were running. Protesters set out for old fishing stations on the Puyallup and Nisqually Rivers south of Seattle in the certain knowledge that they would be arrested. Mel Thom recalled that hundreds of Indians stood on the banks watching apprehensively. "The Indian had been stereotyped to act in certain ways," Thom said. "He was not supposed to take direct action, or to picket, or to demonstrate."

Youth Council leaders brought in outside supporters, including movie star Marlon Brando. Arrested for fishing with a net but released on a technicality, Brando joined some 1,000 Indians and their supporters in a protest march on Olympia, the state capital, where Makah Indians in wolf and whale headdresses staged a war dance on the steps of the capitol rotunda.

The appearance of Brando and, later, of black comedian and activist Dick Gregory focused the attention of the national media on the fish-ins. One of the most widely publicized encounters occurred in October 1965 at Frank's Landing, a favorite Indian fishing spot on the Nisqually River near the Nisqually Reservation, not far from where the old Treaty of Medicine

Policemen in Washington State (left) fire tear gas into a Puyallup encampment during a 1960s fish-in. Nisqually leader Bill Frank Jr. (below) is arrested at another demonstration. Broad media coverage created public awareness of the Indians' early attempts to maintain their traditional fishing rights.

Creek had been signed. Alerted by all the publicity, some 80 uniformed game wardens "came down on us like a sea of green," wrote Laura McCloud, whose parents were participating in the demonstration.

Out on the river, Indians in a dugout canoe lowered their nets. A government powerboat raced out and rammed the canoe, pitching the occupants, including Laura's seven-year-old brother, into the water. On the riverbanks, several persons were injured in a scuffle with law enforcement officials. Laura's father Donald and her mother Janet McCloud—a descendant of Seattle, the famous 19th-century chief of the allied Puget Sound tribes—were among the seven demonstrators arrested. Thanks in part to the news photographs and television film attesting to their rough handling by the game wardens, they won acquittal—and new supporters.

The struggle spread to the Columbia River, where game wardens arrested Yakima fishermen for netting chinook salmon. The Yakimas, who had previously refused to take part in the fish-ins, were outraged and began patrolling the riverbanks carrying rifles. The involvement of this large and politically powerful tribe helped bring the Indians a new ally in their fishing war: the Department of Justice, which intervened in the courts on the side of the Indian fishermen. It was the first time tribal elders could remember that the federal government had stepped in to defend a treaty.

The confrontations continued, however. Some of the most dangerous encounters were initiated by white fishermen who resented the civil dis-

Bill Frank Jr. won the 1992 Albert Schweitzer Prize for Humanitarianism for his work with local governments to ensure the fishing rights of Indians in the Northwest. Indians and white governments are no longer at odds, he declared. "Rather than fighting, we're negotiating. Rather than suing each other, we're combining resources to properly manage the natural resources we all depend on."

obedience of the Indians. Most of the Youth Council activists were gone by then, but one who stayed was Hank Adams, son of an Assiniboin and a Sioux, who had been raised on the Quinault Reservation in Washington State. Adams became the leader in the fight by local tribesmen. Harassed by white vigilantes, he was shot in the stomach while dozing in his car after setting a net in the Puyallup River. Hank Adams survived, and so did the struggle for fishing rights.

Proving that the "Indians had enough guts to stand up," in Mel Thom's words, Adams and the others became catalysts of the new militancy. New organizations proliferated, and Indian activists staged dozens of dramatic events intended to attract national attention. Encouraged by the success of the fish-ins, Indians would go on in the early 1970s to picket museums accused of desecrating Indian bones, block public access to lands they considered Indian property, call attention to advertisements that were demeaning to Indians, and demonstrate against stereotypical movie portrayals by Hollywood and the television networks. They also pressed for Indian studies programs in colleges and universities and documented their grievances in news magazines and books. Echoing the strident calls for Black Power among militants in the civil rights movement, Indian writers began to refer to their own growing sense of self-assurance as Red Power. The phrase was used initially, half in jest, for its shock value. Many Indians disliked the term because of its racial implications and even its political connotations during the Cold War. But it caught on as a catchy shorthand that encapsulated the rising Indian demand for control over their lives.

Behind the drama of Red Power, the old political struggle continued. Tribal leaders, sympathetic churches, and moderate organizations, such as the National Congress of American Indians, lobbied with considerable success in the corridors of the nation's capital to end the termination of reservations, improve education, and enhance self-government. These parallel attacks—militants in the streets, moderates behind the scenes—sometimes reinforced each other. By riveting public attention on an issue, the protests served as a prod to moderate reformers and to the federal government.

LESSONS IN UNITY FOR INDIAN YOUTH

Since 1976, members of an organization called United National Indian Tribal Youth (UNITY) have come together annually to develop their leadership skills in such areas as community service, environment, and health, and to explore ways of applying those skills for the benefit of all Native Americans. In June 1995, San Diego played host to some 1,200 aspiring leaders attending the UNITY Conference, the largest gathering of its kind for American Indian youth.

Conference participants of diverse tribal backgrounds ranging in age from 15 to 24 joined in workshops, cultural exchanges, and dialogues with their elders. The latter impressed on the young people the importance of overcoming the cultural barriers that discouraged tribal groups from making common cause. Indeed, the theme of the 1995 leadership gathering was "Unity Among Nations." In the words of Executive Director J. R. Cook: "The prosperity of Native America depends on all native people working together. Unfortunately, as a people and as individuals we are divided."

At the conclusion of the lively five-day event, the young people issued a declaration of principle. "We stand united to keep the sacred fire of our ancestors burning brightly for ourselves and the future generations," they stated. "We must learn, live, and teach the wisdom and knowledge of our elders."

Young people at the San Diego conference stand behind seated elders, who prepare to bless the council fire that burned throughout the gathering. The youngsters invited elders of various groups to play a role at San Diego and drew inspiration from their example of harmony.

As part of the cultural exchange, native Alaskan girls from the communities of Dillingham and New Stuyahok (top right) perform a Yupik dance entitled "Cauqaga Nauwa," or "My drum, where is it?" In another performance at the gathering, Bonni Cleveland (bottom right) from Tomah, Wisconsin—a member of the Ho Chunk Nation (formerly Winnebago)—depicts a butterfly in artful steps of the Fancy Shawl Dance.

In another group exercise, young people form a talking circle where each member of the circle, or clan, has a chance to address the others on issues of common concern. Afterward, the designated clan leaders came together to write the declaration of principle.

As part of an exercise designed to promote trust and teamwork, a girl relies on a jubilant crowd of supporters to hand her from one side of the room to the other without letting her fall.

Flanked by their advisers, youth leaders from the Navajo reservation town of Chinle, Arizona, proudly display a poster given to them by UNITY members in Oklahoma City. The poster was presented to signify the Arizonans' $750 donation to the American Red Cross following the terrorist bombing of the Alfred P. Murrah Federal Building in Oklahoma City in April 1995.

Following a banquet on the last night of the conference, participants add their individual touches to a mural emblazoned with the symbols and sayings of the many tribal groups represented at the gathering. The mural now hangs at UNITY headquarters in Oklahoma City to commemorate the cooperative spirit of the get-together.

Much of what was achieved resulted from government initiatives aimed at alleviating poverty among Americans generally and not from the concern for the special historic relationship with Indians. In 1961, long before the protests began, tribal governments received a boost in prestige as well as new infusions of money from legislation supported by President John F. Kennedy. The Area Redevelopment Act, which provided loans and grants to help improve pockets of poverty, specifically included 56 Indian reservations. Indian groups and tribal councils, like counties and other local governments, could serve as sponsoring agencies for redevelopment programs and control their planning and funding. New community centers and much-needed infrastructure, such as roads and sewer and water systems, were built. On many reservations, the new buildings replaced outmoded structures erected as part of New Deal make-work programs— or even wooden structures put up during the 19th century.

This breakthrough provided an important precedent when President Lyndon B. Johnson proposed his War on Poverty in 1964. As the Economic Opportunity Act was being shaped on Capitol Hill, 400 Indian leaders met in a nearby Washington hotel under the sponsorship of the Council on Indian Affairs, a traditional coalition of church and other private groups. Largely as a result of the lobbying that took place during and after the conference, tribes were included under all the programs of the Office of Economic Opportunity (OEO) created later that year. The new OEO even provided a special Indian desk to deal directly with tribal grant applications and bypass the regional bureaucracy faced by other applicants.

Tribes immediately began establishing community action agencies to plan, fund, and operate antipoverty programs. All the federal money pouring in seemed too good to be true for some Indians, who feared that their tribes would be billed for the cost of the programs later, as had happened frequently in the past. Wariness soon evaporated, however, and by 1968, no fewer than 129 reservations with a total population of 312,000 people were being served by 63 agencies controlled by the tribes. During that year, $35 million flowed in from OEO for projects ranging from home improvement and job training to work experience for potential teenage dropouts and Head Start for preschool youngsters. In addition, OEO sent to the reservations college-age volunteers from VISTA (Volunteers in Service to America) and the domestic Peace Corps, and set up Job Corps centers to provide vocational training to young adults.

Some reservations also benefited from help supplied by the legal services offices funded by OEO—a necessity at a time when there were scarce-

Navajos on their Arizona reservation learn stonemasonry in order to erect four-cornered houses to replace their traditional hogan design. The Economic Opportunity Act of 1964 enabled Indians for the first time to plan and manage such projects, but the programs did not generate enough jobs to alleviate chronic unemployment on rural reservations.

ly a score of Native American lawyers in the entire United States. In addition to advice on current problems, legal services lawyers established an organization of attorneys devoted solely to issues of Indian jurisprudence, such as fishing rights, termination, and the powers of tribal government. The Native American Rights Fund was developed in 1971 by California Indian Legal Services, an OEO-funded group, with the help of a grant from the Ford Foundation. The Ford Foundation also sponsored a scholarship program aimed at increasing the number of Indian lawyers.

Under the auspices of Johnson's War on Poverty, tribal councils wielded a measure of the power only envisioned during the Indian New Deal of the 1930s. They dealt with a fresh new agency without the tradition of paternalism that frequently marred relations with the Bureau of Indian Affairs. In fact, a central tenet of the War on Poverty called for "maximum feasible participation of the poor." This gave tribes and other agencies the franchise to design their own projects, hire employees with federal funds, and manage day-to-day operations. Hundreds of administrative jobs opened up, luring back college-educated men and women who had forsaken the reservation. With the help of workshops conducted by universities, the new managers learned to carry out functions formerly handled by Indian Bureau employees.

As tribal budgets ballooned—sometimes to $3 or $4 million a year from only $50,000—flaws and factionalism inevitably developed. Nepotism in the distribution of jobs flourished, and a few Indian officials lined

their own pockets. Getting government funds rather than meeting reservation needs too often became the goal. "This grantsmanship business became a disease," wrote Robert Burnette, a prominent Sioux and commissioner of Indian affairs. "Many of our leaders forgot who they were and why they were elected." But the federal money brought hope, jobs, and the possibility of a brighter future. From the rapidly growing group of Indian professionals would emerge a new generation of leaders and entrepreneurs more conventional in style than the young activists but just as committed to Indian self-determination.

The example of OEO paved the way for direct tribal contacts with other federal agencies. Following this lead, the Agriculture, Labor, and other cabinet-level Departments set up their own Indian desks—frequently staffed by Indians—to quickly approve tribes as eligible sponsoring agencies for myriad projects. Through funding from these other departments, reservations saw the construction of industrial parks, resort motels, recreation areas, and thousands of new homes. All this occurred without the direct involvement of the Bureau of Indian Affairs, the agency that traditionally had dispensed and controlled every cent of federal money that reached the reservations.

Tribes reveled in bypassing the bureau. Philip J. Deloria, a Sioux attorney and writer, recalled that in the old days tribal delegations visiting Washington, D.C., spent most of their time in the Indian Bureau. Now they

A Laguna Pueblo youngster prepares to practice the Buffalo Dance as part of a Head Start class in New Mexico. An OEO community action program, Head Start frequently served as a community's first locally run reservation preschool.

were so busy dealing with other government agencies that they had occasion only for a courtesy call: "They would stop by the bureau to say hello to the commissioner on their way back to the airport."

Wary of this new air of independence, bureau officials tried to tighten their grip. In the spring of 1966, Secretary of the Interior Stewart Udall called a meeting of bureau officials in Santa Fe, New Mexico, to map policy. One proposal was a plan to persuade Congress to give the bureau, through the Department of the Interior, control of the antipoverty money that was flowing out to the reservations. The National Congress of American Indians got wind of the meeting and called representatives of 62 tribes to convene in Santa Fe at the same time. After at first barring the door, Udall finally admitted two of these representatives to observe his planning session, a first in bureau history. He gave up on the idea of getting Congress to give the bureau control of OEO funds, but proposed an omnibus bill for the development of tribal natural resources to get Indians "into the economic mainstream."

Udall promised after the meeting that tribal officials would be consulted in shaping the legislation. A few months later, the newly appointed commissioner of Indian affairs, Robert Bennett, an Oneida from Wisconsin, held a series of hearings around the country ostensibly to seek ideas for the bill. Actually the legislation already had been written, and to Bennett's embarrassment, copies of it smuggled out of the bureau. The omnibus bill would have allowed the mortgaging of tribal lands, among other objectionable features. Furious at the failure to consult with them before the measure was written, Indians ridiculed the proposal as the "ominous bill" and "anonymous bill." The measure died in a congressional committee.

Despite its failure to wrest control of the poverty program funds, the bureau still maintained a tight hold on most federal monies spent on the reservations. In 1968 the $35 million in antipoverty funds it had sought to manage amounted to only about one-eighth of the bureau's annual budget for Indian affairs. And it still wielded a power of veto over projects funded by many government agencies. For example, in 1967 the Leech Lake band of Ojibwas came across a plan drawn up by the bureau six years previously recommending development of a recreation area on one of their Minnesota lakes. The Leech Lake Ojibwas updated the plan, took it to the Economic Development Administration, received an initial commitment for funding, and then, without calling attention to the old study, asked the bureau for approval. The bureau called for a study and was told it already had made a study. Then the bureau asked for an update and was told the plan already had been updated. Finally the bureau approved construction of the recreation area but ruled that an access road could not be widened to accommodate trailers because that would infringe upon the rights of whites who had leased Indian-owned land alongside it. And there the plan stalled.

Under increasing pressure from President Johnson, the Indian Bureau loosened up somewhat. In 1968 Johnson sent an unprecedented special message on Indian affairs to Congress in which he urged a "new goal for our Indian programs that stresses self-determination." He appointed a National Council on Indian Opportunity, chaired by Vice President Hubert H. Humphrey, that included Indian leaders and the cabinet members whose agencies dealt with the reservations. The bureau even took a cue from those agencies and began making contracts with a few tribes, trusting them at last to manage and control programs such as schools and road building. By 1970 at least one tribe, the Zuni of New Mexico, had assumed nominal control of their own affairs.

The War on Poverty accomplished much, but it failed to solve the long-term economic problems of the reservations. The devastation caused by allotment and the leasing of Indian lands beginning in the late 19th century had in many cases deprived native peoples of much of their resources and a basis for economic self-sufficiency.

One significant achievement, however, was to help Indians gain a foothold in the field of education, which had been controlled by the Bureau of Indian Affairs for nearly a century. The impetus for community management moved most rapidly among the Navajo. They had the largest reservation in the United States and the biggest population—140,000 residents. In 1966, with financial backing from OEO, the Rough Rock community in Arizona took over operation of a newly constructed $3-million boarding school. Funded by both the bureau and OEO, the Rough Rock Demonstration School became the first Indian boarding school run by Native Americans.

Rough Rock was founded on the principle of intensive community involvement. Local residents comprised the board of trustees. Parents worked as dormitory attendants and were encouraged to participate in summer adult education classes. The school's curriculum was designed to impart the traditional way of life in addition to teaching math, science, and other subjects. Students learned Navajo history and culture from old tribal stories illustrated by Navajo artists. They typically spoke English in most classes, but only after mastering their mother tongue. Navajo leaders invited to evaluate the school reported a "feeling of great pride in the people—pride in what they are doing for their community, pride in what they are doing for their school, and pride in what they are doing for their children."

Rough Rock's success helped spur another pioneering development by the Navajo. In 1968 the tribe started the Navajo Community College, the first institution of higher learning run by Indians for Indians. Despite funds from OEO, the tribe, and private foundations, the new college at first had to share the facilities of the bureau boarding school at Many Farms, 20 miles from Rough Rock. Then, in 1971, a special congressional appropriation allowed construction of a campus in the northern part of the reservation at Tsaile that could accommodate more than 1,000 students.

Both the new campus and its curriculum reflected Navajo heritage. The campus itself was laid out with special emphasis on the traditional four sacred directions. The glass-walled administration building at the center resembled a hogan, the traditional Navajo dwelling. Courses in the two-year college provided for both academic and vocational preparation and included auto mechanics, various agriculture subjects, and secretari-

A Tesuque Pueblo third grader learns numbers in her native tongue as part of the Bilingual Education Act passed in 1968. Its purpose was to help reservation children learn English, but ironically many of them were exposed to their own languages for the first time in such classes.

An aerial view of the Navajo Community College campus reveals a layout based on traditional beliefs. The main entrance of its circular access design is from the sacred easterly direction, and several buildings are constructed in the typical hogan shape. Established in 1968, the school was the first college to be administered by an Indian tribe.

al training. But all students were exposed to courses in Navajo studies, including history, culture, arts and crafts, and language. When the Navajo president of the college, Ned Hatathli, was asked at a news conference to cite what made his college different from other two-year institutions, he replied wryly, "Well, we don't teach that Columbus discovered America."

Navajos retained tight control over the college. The board of regents included the tribal chairman, five members representing reservation agencies, and the student body president. An advisory board of faculty members, students, and administrators excluded non-Indians, who made up about two-thirds of the faculty. The school's first president, Dr. Robert Roessel, a white man, was urged to step aside after one year of service even though his wife Ruth was Navajo—and architect of the college's celebrated Navajo studies program—and he himself was an advocate of Indian self-determination. "This is an Indian-owned and an Indian-operated institution," said his successor, Ned Hatathli, "and we certainly don't want any people other than Indian to dictate to us what is good for us."

In the decade following the founding of the Navajo Community College, some two dozen other primarily two-year institutions were established. They bridged the West from Michigan to California and from Arizona to North Dakota and served each of Montana's seven reservations and North Dakota's four reservations. Subsidized largely by appropriations under the Tribally Controlled Community College Act of 1978, they enrolled more than 10,000 Indians full- and part-time and contributed to an extraordinary growth in opportunity. In 1960 the number of Indians in attendance at all U.S. colleges was only about 2,000; by the early 1970s, that figure had burgeoned to 40,000.

Other advances sought to improve the impoverished state of public schools, which enrolled two-thirds of all Indian children who went to school. The Elementary and Secondary Education Act of 1965 and subsequent amendments targeted the special needs of all low-income American children, including Indians. During a decade in which Indian attendance nearly doubled in public schools and boarding and day schools, these measures provided increased funds for adult vocational training and bilingual education. Although bilingual teaching was adopted to help Indian youngsters learn English, some learned their native tongue in the process.

Later, in 1969, the work of the Senate Special Subcommittee on Indian Education spotlighted the problems of Indians attending public schools. Under the chairmanship of Robert F. Kennedy and, after his assassination, his brother Edward, the panel conducted hearings producing 4,077 pages of testimony. Citing woeful shortcomings in buildings and teachers, and dropout rates twice the national average, the subcommittee report concluded that "our national policies for educating American Indians are a failure of major proportions." Out of this investigation emerged the Indian Education Act of 1972, which provided increased grants to public schools with Indian students, promoted bilingual education, and encouraged parental and community participation.

Legislation that was intended to benefit Indians sometimes failed to recognize their unique status. One such controversial by-product of the congressional emphasis on equality was the Indian Civil Rights Act of 1968. Indians welcomed the part of this measure that effectively repealed the termination-era legislation that had permitted states to assume civil and criminal jurisdiction over reservations. This provision, which allowed for state jurisdiction only with tribal permission, strengthened tribal courts. Other provisions extended some constitutional guarantees of the Bill of Rights to the relationship between individual Indians and their tribal governments—an action many Indians saw as a threat to tribal sovereignty and an imposition of white legal concepts on the traditional relationship between an individual tribal member and the larger group.

Young activists saw few real benefits coming out of Washington, D.C., during this period. They objected to government bureaucrats controlling the purse strings and to most of the decisions made in the poverty programs. Clyde Warrior, a Ponca from Oklahoma and president in 1967 of the National Indian Youth Council, spoke caustically of "packaged programs wheeled into Indian communities by outsiders" and derided government references to grass-roots democracy as a "slick job of salesmanship." Warrior pointed out that younger Indians were even less willing to work within the system. "Those of us who headed the movement five years ago now are considered Uncle Tomahawks," he warned. "There is a more and more angry bunch of kids coming up."

By 1969 Indian discontent was reaching a boil among both young and old in the San Francisco area. The campuses at San Francisco State University and the University of California at Berkeley were already simmering with demonstrations protesting racial discrimination and the war in Vietnam. Young Indians joined these protests and demonstrated successfully for creation of special departments devoted to Indian studies. At the same time, a more ambitious and dramatic protest was being discussed: the occupation of the little island of Alcatraz, site of the federal penitentiary known as "The Rock."

Some Indians already had attempted to take over this 22-acre chunk of stone in San Francisco Bay. In 1964, the year after its cellblocks were abandoned, five Sioux men occupied the island for four hours before being ousted by U.S. marshals. The wife of one of them, Belva Cottier, had planned the invasion, basing it on her interpretation of the Fort Laramie treaty of 1868. According to that treaty, any parcel of federal land taken from the Indians and then abandoned reverted to the Indians.

A federal court suit based on this interpretation was dismissed, but the idea of occupying Alcatraz to dramatize the plight of all Indians did not disappear. It came to the fore again in the fall of 1969 when the San Francisco Indian Center, a popular gathering place for Bay Area Indians, was destroyed by fire. Older leaders decided Alcatraz would be their new cultural center, and they began recruiting Indian college students to invade it. On November 9, in a trial run, five young men swam ashore from a

The Navajo Preparatory School class of 1995 poses for a graduation picture in Farmington, New Mexico. All 38 graduates of the small, college-preparatory school founded by the Navajo Nation Council in 1991 planned to attend institutions of higher learning.

borrowed Canadian clipper ship and temporarily claimed The Rock before being turned away by authorities. Permanent occupation began on November 20, when 78 students landed, posted a sign reading "You Are Now on Indian Land," and set up housekeeping in the old cellblocks. The invaders expected opposition but were surprised to find the island's government caretaker bringing coffee and an offer from his wife to share their shower and toilet facilities.

Under the name Indians of All Tribes, the group issued a proclamation "To the Great White Father and All His People." An ironic statement of their motives and intentions, it claimed the island "in the name of all American Indians by right of discovery." This wording was an allusion to the earliest

rationale by which the old imperial powers—Spain, France, and England—had gained a foothold in North America. Offering to purchase the island for $24 "in glass beads and red cloth," as the Dutch had bought Manhattan, the proclamation pointed out that Alcatraz was "more than suitable as an Indian Reservation." It also enumerated the resemblances between the desolate island and the typical reservation, including the lack of running water, healthcare facilities, productive soil, and industry. The most telling resemblance was the reference to the island's former occupants: "The population has always been held as prisoners and kept dependent on others." The proclamation concluded by setting forth the occupiers' hope to convert the island into a cultural and spiritual center, university, and museum—with the help of federal dollars.

The island of Alcatraz (above), site of a former federal prison, looms like a huge rock in San Francisco Bay. From November 1969 to June 1971, Indians occupied the abandoned island, claiming squatters' rights under the terms of the 1868 Treaty of Fort Laramie. At left, the Golden Gate Bridge serves as a backdrop for a tipi erected on the island.

The federal government responded cautiously to the takeover. The new administration of President Richard M. Nixon, intent upon avoiding confrontation, sought to settle the matter through negotiation. The new commissioner of Indian affairs, Louis R. Bruce, the son of a Mohawk and

Indian squatters on Alcatraz wait at wharfside to receive a boatload of supplies. The protesters, who called themselves Indians of All Tribes, relied heavily on sympathetic volunteers to contribute and transport food, water, and equipment such as electric generators by boat across the tricky bay waters.

a Sioux, openly sympathized with the demonstrators, but negotiations were controlled directly from the White House. Government representatives turned down the Indian demand for a college and cultural center, maintaining that it was "unreasonable and unrealistic, primarily because the island does not lend itself to any high-density proposal." They offered instead to turn Alcatraz into a national park (the eventual outcome), but with an Indian theme and staffed primarily by Native Americans. The people on Alcatraz flatly rejected that and other proposals, which included an Indian amusement park. Something of the distance and distrust between the two sides became clear when a federal negotiator visited the island: He refused to drink the coffee offered by his hosts because he feared it had been laced with LSD.

The occupation of Alcatraz proved to be a masterstroke of political theater. First came a blitz of national media coverage of the Indian demands. Then came shipments of food and water from mainland churches and other organizations to help overcome a temporary blockade erected by the Coast Guard; on that first Thanksgiving Day, a major restaurant in San Francisco donated cooked turkeys. And hundreds of Indians from all over the country poured in to visit or to take up residence on the island; at one time or another, people from no fewer than 50 tribes lived on Alcatraz.

Many came out of a commitment to Red Power. LaNada Boyer, a Bannock-Shoshone and a leader in the fight to launch an Indian studies curriculum on the Berkeley campus, spent a year on the island. "I commuted back and forth to the university with my two-year-old son," she wrote. "We would hitchhike and then catch a sailboat or a speedboat to the island. I wrote all the public relations proposals that were released from the island. I then turned in some of their material for the work that I was doing in my classes."

Others came out of curiosity and were converted. "Alcatraz was the catalyst," recalled Grace Thorpe, the daughter of the storied Indian athlete, Jim Thorpe, a Sauk and Fox. "It made me put my furniture into storage and spend my life savings." George Horse Capture, a Gros Ventre who worked as a steel inspector, read about Alcatraz in the newspaper and volunteered to spend weekends on the island with his young sons helping unload supplies. Rediscovering his roots, he then enrolled in college to learn skills that would help his people. For him and thousands of other Indians, he recalled: "Alcatraz tapped into something. It was the lance that burst the boil."

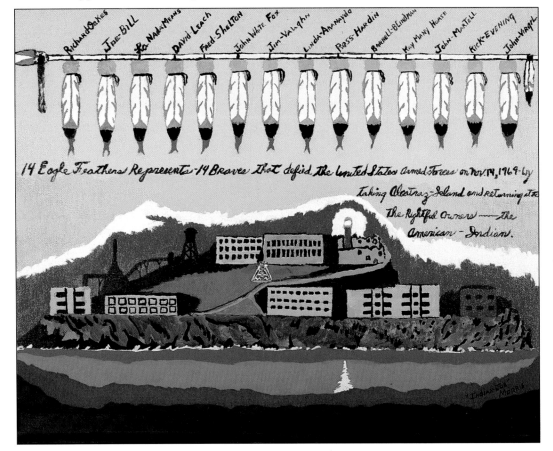

A painting by "Indian Joe" Morris, the mainland coordinator for the Alcatraz occupiers, depicts a stylized landscape of the island along with 14 eagle feathers designating the names of the original occupying group. Morris, an experienced longshoreman, taught boat handling to the volunteers who shipped supplies to Alcatraz.

Richard Oakes, a Mohawk, the chief spokesman for the Alcatraz protesters, unloads supplies from a truck on the island. He is helped by his stepdaughter, Yvonne, who died after a tragic fall in one of the island's buildings. The occupation of Alcatraz became a symbol of Indian unity and brought worldwide attention to the Indians' grievances.

The population on the island, which once soared to 1,000 but typically numbered about 100, settled in for the long haul. They organized a school for the children and assigned everyone a job in work sections ranging from security to sanitation. Meals were taken communally inside the main cellblock. Powwows featuring various tribal dances helped sustain morale. One morning, a rock band showed up, towed from the mainland on a barge carrying used car batteries to power their electronics. The island even had its own radio transmitter, which broadcast a signal to the mainland, where it was picked up by the Pacifica network and relayed to regular stations. For 15 minutes on weekday evenings, Radio Free Alcatraz broadcast music, information on Indian history, and the latest proclamation from the island's elected seven-member council.

The most prominent member of the council in the early weeks was a Mohawk named Richard Oakes. A charismatic student organizer at San Francisco State, Oakes was powerfully built with a shock of black hair and sculptured good looks. After he led his fellow students ashore at Alcatraz, he became the spokesman most sought after by the media. By the beginning of 1970, however, a power struggle had developed between Oakes's mostly student group and a group of unemployed, older Indians—many of them with drug or alcohol problems—who began to replace students who were returning to college. Among the issues were media

Members of a group called Indians of All Tribes demonstrate at the main entrance of Fort Lawton, Seattle, during their occupation of the surplus U.S. Army post in the spring of 1970. Eventually, through lobbying efforts, they were able to build a cultural center on 20 acres of the fort's land, which they leased for 99 years.

attention and control of the thousands of dollars being donated to the cause. This struggle was soon overshadowed when Oakes's young step-daughter accidentally fell four stories down an open stairwell in the for-mer guards' quarters, suffering fatal injuries.

Oakes and his family left the island, and their departure seemed to mark the beginning of a long decline. The Indians lingered month after month, but the media and general public lost interest. Alcohol and drugs, which had been discouraged by the original occupation force, became commonplace on Alcatraz. Some on the island fought with one another, brandished weapons, and set fire to buildings. The population shrank after the government cut off electricity, telephone service, and water. White House aides decided negotiations "should be allowed to fade out." Finally, on June 11, 1971—some 19 months after the Indians took back Alcatraz—a score of heavily armed U.S. marshals landed on the island. They escorted back to the mainland what remained of the occupation force: six men, four women, and five children.

Alcatraz already had served as the catalyst for dozens of attempted occupations of federal property. Among the favorite targets were region-al offices of the Bureau of Indian Affairs. In Michigan, Ojibwas in war paint and ceremonial garb laid claim to an abandoned federal lighthouse along Lake Superior. In northern California, Pit River Indians, refusing a government offer of forty-seven cents an acre for more than three million acres lost a century before, joined with veterans of the Alcatraz occupa-tion and repeatedly tried to take back some of their land. And in New York Harbor, Indian demonstrators failed in their attempt to gain a foothold on another history-laden little landmass—Ellis Island, the former gateway for millions of European immigrants.

While these protests raised the consciousness of Indians and prodded the consciences of non-Indians, they rarely resulted in a substantive pay-off. Demonstrations evidenced a scattershot range of aims—from a demand for restoration of lands to a simple protest against bureau paternalism—and seldom focused on follow-up negotiations or legislation to achieve specific outcomes.

A remarkable exception occurred in Seattle. During the spring of 1970, a group of Indians petitioned the local authorities for permission to establish an Indian cultural center on a portion of Fort Lawton, an army post soon to be declared surplus and turned over to the city. After being ignored by officials, some of the Indians took matters into their own hands and moved onto the property. They were ejected by military policemen, however, and each subsequent attempt to occupy the post was repelled. Many demonstrators were jailed or injured in angry scuffles. Then, after setting up a tipi encampment near the main gate, the protesters switched tactics and began a prolonged lobbying campaign that won the support of many local organizations. Negotiations with the federal

The cultural center complex located at Fort Lawton is a contemporary Indian design featuring giant cedar timbers in its construction, both inside and out. Called the Daybreak Star Indian Cultural Center and Gallery, it was dedicated on May 13, 1977.

government and the city led to an agreement in November 1971 to lease 20 acres of old Fort Lawton to the newly formed United Indians of All Tribes Foundation. Construction then began in 1975 on the foundation's headquarters—funded by the federal government, the city, and three tribes: the Colville, Quinault, and Makah. This was the first step in a master plan for development of a heritage center, library, performing arts center, and other facilities. The complex was completed and dedicated in 1977.

During this period of discontent, President Nixon proved to be extremely sympathetic to Indians. Even before his inauguration, he asked Alvin M. Josephy Jr., a historian well respected by Native Americans, to prepare a special report suggesting changes in policy. Nixon acted on many of Josephy's recommendations. He gave tribal leaders direct access to the White House by assigning the aide to one of his top domestic advisers as a full-time troubleshooter for Indian complaints. The Sioux-Mohawk Louis Bruce, Nixon's commissioner of Indian affairs, shook up the hidebound bureaucracy by appointing a dozen young Indians to key policymaking posts. These appointees pushed Nixon's program to give tribal councils greater control over their own affairs.

Nixon's policies and his restraint during the Alcatraz occupation surprised and pleased many Indians, although they were perplexed by his motivations. Some speculated that his pro-Indian stance was purely political, an attempt to attract votes from at least one minority at a time when blacks generally opposed his administration. Perhaps a more telling possibility was Nixon's enormous admiration for his old football coach at Whittier College, Wallace Newman. A Luiseño Indian whom the players affectionately called "Chief," Newman was a former all-American player at the University of Southern California and, by Nixon's testimony, second only to Nixon's own father in his influence on the young man. Nixon later wrote of the lesson he had learned from Newman as a scrawny substitute player with great passion but little gift for the game: ". . . that when you lose you don't quit, that when you lose you fight harder the next time."

Whatever Nixon's motivation, indeed he presided over a period of constructive legislation for Indians. The first major step was the restoration of the sacred lands and waters of the Taos Pueblo. These mountainous lands encompass Blue Lake, a stunningly beautiful body of water nestled high up in a bowl on a 12,000-foot mountain. For centuries before the arrival of the Spaniards, Blue Lake had been an important source of irrigation water and a vital shrine for an annual pilgrimage. In 1906, without even consulting its owners, the federal government took away the area and incorporated it into Carson National Forest. The Indians fought for more than six decades to get it back, basing their plea on religious grounds and refusing all offers of monetary compensation. Finally, with Nixon's strong backing and support from tribes throughout the country, Congress in 1970 authorized the return of the lake and 48,000 surrounding acres.

Nixon moved to right other old wrongs. After the Blue Lake restoration, two other tribes successfully petitioned for the return of lands: the Yakima in Washington for Mount Adams and the Warm Springs Indians of Oregon for some

Vice President Richard M. Nixon wears tribal regalia presented to him on the occasion of his visit to the Fort Berthold Reservation, North Dakota, in 1960. Ten years later, as president, Nixon made it a priority to promote financial aid for Indians, return some of their lands, and foster Indian self-determination.

60,000 acres. These were the first of such restorations that were granted without the tribes having to engage in prolonged and costly legislative or court battles. The administration also pushed through legal recognition of aboriginal rights in Alaska, which, unlike those in the lower United States, had never been extinguished by treaty. The Alaska Native Claims Settlement Act of 1971 granted people of Indian, Eskimo, and Aleut ancestry nearly $1 billion and 44 million acres of land—about 12 percent of the state—to settle all aboriginal land claims. Native individuals became shareholders in 12 regional corporations and more than 200 village corporations set up by the legislation to control both the land and the money.

What won the most plaudits for Nixon was his position on termination. This policy of severing the trustee relationship between tribes and the federal government had been imposed by Congress under the Eisenhower administration, which Nixon served as vice president. Termination had lost favor with every chief executive since then, but none denounced it with Nixon's precision or passion. In his special message to Congress in July 1970, he set the tone for his Indian policy by calling for self-

In 1971 Menominee tribal members protest the 1954 act that terminated their status as an Indian nation and converted their reservation lands to county property. The Menominee lobbied successfully to reverse the law, thus reclaiming their status as a tribe along with their property rights.

Responding to the threat to her tribe's well-being, Ada Deer was instrumental in organizing the successful lobby for the repeal of the 1954 Menominee Termination Act. The Menominee's tribal status was restored by Congress in December 1973.

determination without termination. "The time has come to break decisively with the past and to create the conditions for a new era in which the Indian future is determined by Indian acts and Indian decisions," he said. "We must make it clear that Indians can become independent of federal control without being cut off from federal concern and federal support."

When he spoke, a significant test of Nixon's resolve was already taking shape among members of the first tribe to be terminated, the Menominee. Before their termination took effect in 1961, cutting off the federal trustee relationship and converting their reservation into a county, the 3,500 Menominees in northern Wisconsin constituted one of the most self-sufficient tribes in the United States. After termination, their fortunes plummeted. By 1967 the county had become the poorest in the state and was in danger of losing its lakefront land when a group of Menominee dissidents organized a grass-roots movement known as DRUMS—the acronym for Determination of Rights and Unity for Menominee Shareholders—and began making noise. "There comes a certain time in history when certain ideas are ready to be acted on," said Ada Deer, one of the main organizers, "and now is the time for reversing termination."

Other Menominees were less optimistic about the tribe's ability to undo termination and regain their tribal identity. "Intermarriage trends will make assimilation of the tribe inevitable anyway," one Indian argued. "Menominees can't really go back, but must learn to live and adapt in white

man's society. Not only is the dilution of Menominee blood a factor, but also Menominees like many of the amenities of white man's culture, e.g., car, phone, TV, etc. Menominees aren't about to give these things up."

But the DRUMS leaders were undeterred. They employed a number of the confrontational tactics of the Red Power movement. They picketed the land sales office, organized a 220-mile march on the state capital, Madison, and made skillful use of the media. But they also put up candidates and organized the shareholders so successfully that in 1972 DRUMS supporters took control of the overall trust and the corporation. They halted the land sales and then, encouraged by President Nixon's stated opposition to termination as well as strong backing from Wisconsin's elected officials, academic community, and most of the state newspapers, launched a national lobbying campaign to restore their tribe to federal trust status. They solicited the support of other Indians across the nation and won the endorsement of more than 15 Indian organizations and tribes.

Their argument had two basic themes. First, the DRUMS leaders provided evidence proving that termination had harmed rather than helped Menominee progress toward self-sufficiency. Secondly, they argued that Congress, by correcting the situation, could send a message to all Native Americans that the United States's political system could actually be made to work as a tool to help Indians safeguard their cultures. In order to enlist support for their cause in Washington, Ada Deer, who two decades later would be appointed head of the Indian Bureau, learned to lobby with a light touch. She remembered making her way through the bureau's headquarters passing out candy to "sweeten up" officials and win their backing.

With support from other tribes, Indian Bureau officials, politicians in both parties, and, above all, strong backing from the Nixon White House, Ada Deer and her fellow Menominees prevailed. In 1973 Congress voted overwhelmingly to reverse the Menominee Termination Act and restore the tribe to full trust status, with all its previous treaty rights, federal benefits, and practically all of the former reservation. This same "clear reversal of a policy which was wrong," in Nixon's words, soon was won by a number of groups that had been terminated: the Confederated Tribes of Siletz Indians in Oregon, the Wyandot, Peoria, and Ottawa tribes of Oklahoma, and certain bands of Paiutes in Utah.

In spite of his positive actions, President Nixon failed to defuse the anger of the Red Power militants. One reason was that his administration generally refused to consult with them, preferring to deal instead with the more moderate elected leaders from the reservations. To cultivate loyalty and support, the White House even subsidized an organization of such representatives, the National Tribal Chairmen's Association. The association frequently condemned confrontation tactics. Its members, in turn, were denounced by other Indians as pawns of the federal government.

The most radical group to emerge during this period was the American Indian Movement (AIM). A product of the burgeoning urbanization process—nearly half the Indian population now lived in cities—AIM was founded in Minneapolis in 1968 by a small group of Ojibwas concerned about discrimination, lack of job opportunities, and, especially, relationships with the police. Some of them were former prison inmates, with little patience for picketing and other low-key means of civil disobedience, and they modeled their organization loosely after the Black Panthers. To prevent mistreatment of Indians arrested for drunkenness, AIM mounted a nightly car patrol armed with two-way radios, cameras, and tape recorders. The AIM presence not only sharply reduced instances of police brutality but also lowered the unusually high number of Indians arrested for public intoxication.

AIM expanded its operations to other cities, winning a reputation as the "shock troops of Indian sovereignty." Its key leaders were Dennis Banks, one of the Ojibwa founders, and an Oglala Sioux whom he recruited named Russell Means. Born on the Pine Ridge Reservation but raised mostly in Oakland, California, Means had knocked around as a rodeo hand and as a student at five different colleges. Tall and handsome, he flaunted his Indian identity by wearing long braids, turquoise jewelry, an embroidered vest, and boots. Means possessed what a fellow Sioux described as a "bizarre knack for staging demonstrations that attracted the sort of press coverage Indians had been looking for." Inspired by Means and by the Indian takeover of Alcatraz, AIM seized the replica of the *Mayflower* at Plymouth Rock on Thanksgiving Day 1970, and the following

Nish Two Suns, an organizer for the American Indian Movement, speaks to Indians in Farmington, New Mexico, in 1974 to rally support for AIM among the tribes of the Southwest. AIM was founded in Minneapolis in 1968 in order to combat police mistreatment of urban Indians.

year staged a temporary occupation of the Mount Rushmore National Memorial in South Dakota, camping atop the carved granite busts of George Washington, Thomas Jefferson, Abraham Lincoln, and Theodore Roosevelt.

AIM members also started forging ties with the reservations that they had left early in life. They organized a highly successful protest by reservation dwellers early in 1972 after a 51-year-old Oglala cowboy named Raymond Yellow Thunder had been humiliated and murdered by drunken whites in the off-reservation town of Gordon, Nebraska. Means and Banks led an auto caravan of 1,300 Indians, mostly Sioux, from the Pine Ridge and Rosebud Reservations into Gordon. Marching the streets of the town for three days with drums beating and red flags flying, they made certain that local authorities brought the killers to justice.

Although their show of force in Gordon gained many new supporters on the Sioux reservations, a venture later that spring in Banks's native territory backfired. An AIM contingent showed up uninvited on the Ojibwa's Leech Lake Reservation in Minnesota to help enforce the tribe's treaty fishing rights. But when AIM members began talking of a violent confrontation with white fishermen, publicly brandishing weapons, and setting up roadblocks, the tribal council ordered them to leave.

In the autumn of 1972, AIM joined eight other Indian organizations in sponsoring the Trail of Broken Treaties. This demonstration to dramatize Indian demands consisted of automobile caravans beginning on the West Coast, moving through the western reservations to pick up more protesters, and arriving in the nation's capital on the eve of the presidential election. The event was given urgency by several recent unexplained violent

78

THE COLOSSUS OF CRAZY HORSE

In 1947 sculptor Korczak Ziolkowski, who had helped chisel the faces of four presidents atop Mount Rushmore, embarked on an even larger task 17 miles away. At the request of Sioux chiefs, he set out to transform the granite summit of Thunderhead Mountain into a statue of the great war chief Crazy Horse, seated on horseback with arm pointing to the southeast and the sacred Black Hills he had fought valiantly to preserve for the Lakota.

Relying entirely on private contributions to finance the nonprofit project, the sculptor worked for many years, using dynamite and a jackhammer to chip away at the rock. Following his death in 1982, members of his family continued the mammoth undertaking. By 1995 more than 8 million tons of granite had been removed from the mountain, and the great face of Crazy Horse was beginning to take shape.

Korczak Ziolkowski and Henry Standing Bear, a Brulé Sioux chief, stand before a model of the Crazy Horse sculpture during the dedication of the site on June 3, 1948. The chief invited Korczak, who went by his first name, to create the world's largest mountain carving so whites would know that Indians have "great heroes, too."

Korczak's scale model, shown here against the massive backdrop of the work in progress, reveals how the sculpture will look when completed. Crazy Horse is pointing toward the hills on the horizon, where as he put it, "my dead lie buried."

Dwarfed by the 87-foot-high granite face of Crazy Horse, participants in the annual June hike reach the summit of Thunderhead Mountain—the only occasion on which people can actually walk on the mountain carving. Korczak obtained the site in a land exchange with the federal government.

USA 13c

Crazy Horse

This Crazy Horse stamp, issued by the U.S. Postal Service in 1982 as part of its "Great Americans" series, was patterned after Korczak's scale model of the war chief, who contributed mightily to the annihilation of Custer's forces at Little Bighorn in 1876 and was killed a year later while resisting arrest.

Indians stand their ground outside the Bureau of Indian Affairs building in Washington, D.C., which they forcibly occupied on November 2, 1972, to protest federal government policies concerning Native Americans. The protesters renamed the building the Native American Embassy.

A woman demonstrates her hostility to the government by wearing an inverted American flag in the occupied BIA auditorium. Some 500 activists remained in the building for a week before walking away without incident.

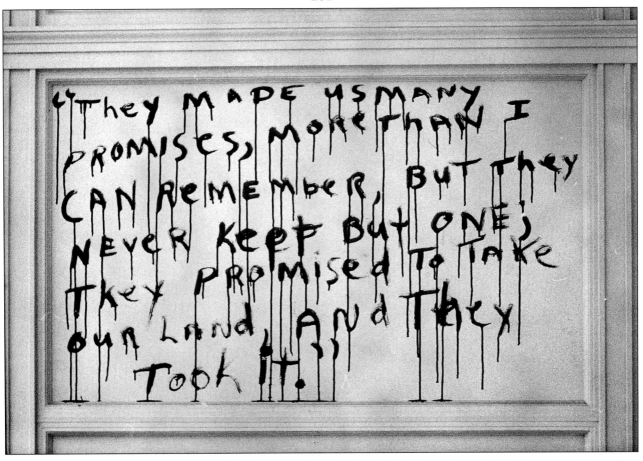

"They made us many promises, more than I can remember, but they never kept but one; they promised to take our land, and they took it."

On a wall of the BIA building, the Indians painted this famous quotation—from a 19th-century Sioux warrior—that acidly assesses the relationship between whites and Native Americans.

deaths across the nation, including that of Alcatraz leader Richard Oakes, who was shot to death in California. The caravans carried to Washington some 2,000 Indians and a list of demands to present to the White House.

The so-called Twenty Points, written largely by the fish-in leader Hank Adams, proposed a radical redefinition of United States-Indian affairs. The document demanded a return to the time more than a century before when treaties constituted the basis for relations between tribes and the federal government. The very first point called for restoration of governmental treaty-making authority, which had been ended by Congress in 1871. The second point urged establishment of a commission to make new treaties with tribes. Other points called for treaty relations as the standard for governing all Indians, abolition of the Indian Bureau, and increasing the Indian land base to 110 million acres. It was a thoughtful if politically unacceptable document, but the Twenty Points got swallowed up in the rapid-fire swirl of events after the caravans reached Washington.

The trouble began in a dispute over accommodations. Caravan leaders thought that rooms had been arranged in advance with the help of the Indian Bureau, but the bureau had been ordered by the White House not to cooperate. When sufficient accommodations were not available, the AIM contingent led angry protesters in a takeover of bureau headquarters, ousting police who attempted to intervene. Indians occupied the building for a week, certain that the cordon of police and U.S. marshals

During a siege at Wounded Knee on the Pine Ridge Reservation in South Dakota, well-armed Indians stand guard at the Sacred Heart Catholic Church. Mounting tensions between local Sioux and an opposing faction of mostly AIM members came to a head in February 1973. U.S. marshals and the FBI were called in to restore order, and a 72-day stand-off ensued.

would attack at any moment. The White House had no intention of letting that happen, but in anticipation of an assault, the protesters ripped apart the building and its furnishings to build barricades.

The coolest head among the demonstrators, Hank Adams, negotiated with White House officials. He agreed to end the occupation in return for a promise not to prosecute the occupants and to give the Twenty Points serious consideration. The White House later rejected all the demands and fired Louis Bruce, the Indian commissioner who had shown sympathy with the occupation by spending a night inside the headquarters. But by then AIM leaders had walked away from the scene carrying boxes of official files that they mistakenly thought would document bureau corruption. They left several million dollars worth of damages, but the government imposed no penalty, and even paid their way home: $66,000 for travel expenses was part of the settlement negotiated by Adams.

AIM's adventures grew more flamboyant. In February 1973, about 200 members staged a demonstration outside the courthouse in Custer, South Dakota, in the Black Hills west of the Pine Ridge Reservation. They came at the request of Sarah Bad Heart Bull, an Oglala Sioux, because she rightly feared that the white killer of her son, Wesley, would escape justice. Outside the courthouse where a hearing in the case was taking place, a melee broke out between police and Indians. The courthouse and two patrol

Wary federal authorities patrol the perimeters of the sealed-off village in an armored personnel carrier. Despite efforts to avoid confrontation, by the end of the siege two Indians had been killed and a U.S. marshal was permanently paralyzed.

cars were set afire, an abandoned building was burned down, and 27 Indians were arrested. One of them was Mrs. Bad Heart Bull, who served five months in jail while her son's killer went free. From Custer, AIM moved on to set up new headquarters in Rapid City, a town many Indians considered the most anti-Indian in America. A scuffle broke out in a bar. Some 25 whites were hospitalized and 41 Indians arrested.

AIM was already embroiled in the mounting turmoil on the Pine Ridge Reservation. The reservation, with its 12,000 Oglala Sioux, was in the poorest county in the United States, and more than half of its work force lacked steady employment. Russell Means, who had lived most of his life in cities, had taken up residence there to study the old sacred ways with Oglala medicine men. He started a purchasing cooperative, condemned the tribal chairman as a puppet of the Indian Bureau, and made public his intention to run for the job. The tribal chairman, Richard Wilson, in turn, denounced AIM and obtained an order from the reservation's court forbidding AIM members from speaking at, or even attending, public meetings on the reservation. To show he meant business, Wilson had Means arrested for addressing a meeting after his return from occupying the Indian Bureau headquarters in Washington.

Even without AIM to stir the pot, enough strife already beset the reservation. According to his many opponents, Wilson had won the chairman's

A burned-out car surrounded by trash represents the ruins at Wounded Knee following the siege. After lengthy negotiations, including efforts on behalf of the National Council of Churches, the occupiers withdrew peacefully.

post the previous spring only by buying votes. He was accused of doling out jobs to relatives and friends and diverting federal grants their way. Wilson's conduct reopened old wounds on a reservation with a large population of Oglalas who had never been reconciled to the type of elected tribal government introduced during the Indian New Deal of the 1930s. When these Indians organized and tried to impeach Wilson, he responded with threats and intimidation. To help him maintain order and prevent organized protests by AIM, the Indian Bureau gave Wilson $62,000 to form a so-called Tribal Ranger Force. These auxiliaries called themselves the Guardians of the Oglala Nation—"Goon Squad," for short—and took pride in terrorizing Wilson's political opponents.

The breaking point for the anti-Wilson group came in late February 1973, not long after AIM's venture into the town of Custer. Wilson's opponents were attempting to impeach him for the second time, and the Indian Bureau selected Wilson himself to conduct the proceedings. The federal government also sent in 65 heavily armed U.S. marshals to make sure that order prevailed around bureau headquarters in the village of Pine Ridge. When the impeachment vote predictably failed, the anti-Wilson forces invited AIM onto the reservation and asked them to set up a rump government. The site they chose had enormous symbolic and historical significance: the hamlet of Wounded Knee, where more than 200 of their ancestors had been gunned down by the U.S. Army in 1890.

AIM leaders Russell Means, holding a drumstick at left, and Dennis Banks, in vest, celebrate the dismissal of charges against them in connection with the Wounded Knee siege.

The AIM caravan of 54 cars carrying 250 Indians arrived in Wounded Knee on the evening of February 27, 1973. They shot out the few street lights illuminating the tiny cluster of buildings, ransacked the trading post for guns and ammunition, and set up roadblocks. On the perimeter around an old Catholic church, they began digging bunkers. Within the next day, they faced a small army of federal marshals, 250 FBI agents, and bureau police, some equipped with M-16 rifles and armored personnel carriers, who moved up and surrounded Wounded Knee. Both sides opened fire, and the siege of Wounded Knee began.

Periodic truces and negotiations punctuated the siege. On March 11,

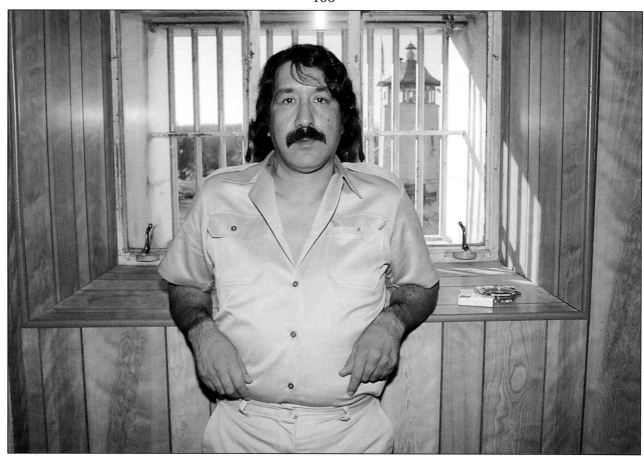

anti-Wilson Sioux who had made their way through the lines joined with the occupiers in the proclamation of the new Independent Oglala Nation. Leaders called for abolition of the hated Wilson government and federal recognition of rights guaranteed under the 1868 Fort Laramie treaty—a demand that would require Congress to recognize Sioux sovereignty over no less than all of western South Dakota and large parts of three other states. Afterward, the Oglala Nation's spiritual leader, Leonard Crow Dog, conducted the old Ghost Dance for the occupiers. It was this shuffling dance, which purported to make the white man go away, revive the Indian dead, and restore the old ways, that had set the stage for the Wounded Knee massacre in 1890.

Never before, not even during the long occupation of Alcatraz, had the proponents of Red Power enjoyed such a prominent national platform. The media converged on this armed confrontation at a site recently made poignantly familiar in Dee Brown's best-selling book, *Bury My Heart at Wounded Knee*. Searchlights and tracer shells and flares fired by the government forces lent a surrealistic air to the siege as they lighted up the night sky. Government planes and helicopters buzzed overhead, and organizations supporting the occupiers sent small aircraft of their own to parachute in food and medical supplies. Members of 64 different tribes, along with sympathetic non-Indians, showed up at one time or another to share the bunkers with AIM. The National Council of Churches even sent

Former AIM leader Leonard Peltier was sentenced to two consecutive life terms for the murder of two FBI agents during a 1975 showdown at Pine Ridge. Controversy envelops the case; by the mid-1990s, Peltier had become an international cause célèbre for many who feel that he is innocent and was unfairly tried.

in representatives who promised to stand between the lines and prevent an assault by the government forces. Wilson's supporters, who set up their own roadblocks, were itching for just such an all-out attack, but the White House had issued strict orders against one.

The siege went on, probably too long for the most effective propaganda impact. Even as the periodic firefights took their toll—two Indians dead, a U.S. marshal partially paralyzed, and other wounded on both sides—Wounded Knee became an old story, and media interest waned. On May 8, on the advice of local Sioux who had been talking with government negotiators, AIM abandoned Wounded Knee.

Remarkably little came of the 72-day standoff. White House representatives told the anti-Wilson forces that only Congress had the authority to do anything about the 1868 treaty—and almost certainly would not. The government arrested 562 persons in connection with Wounded Knee, but only 15 were convicted, almost all on minor charges such as trespassing. Richard Wilson remained in power, narrowly defeating Russell Means in 1974 amid charges of wholesale fraud. Plagued by the lack of a program to effect real change, AIM went into decline, hounded by the FBI, which had infiltrated the organization. AIM's fatal flaw, a Sioux lawyer later said, was its "preference for publicity over policy."

The long confrontation at Wounded Knee culminated the decade-long rise of the Red Power movement. The protests had aroused in many a new sense of cultural identity and self-respect and had sensitized government officials and many other non-Indians to conditions on the reservations. But tangible progress typically resulted only when the protests and demonstrations had a clear purpose and were followed up by a carefully prepared legislative effort or litigation.

Perhaps no issue illustrated this more effectively than the fish-ins that had launched the Red Power movement. In February 1974, just 10 months after the end of the Wounded Knee standoff, the fish-ins begun by the Washington tribes a decade earlier led to a milestone legal decision. Federal judge George Boldt reaffirmed their special tribal fishing rights under the old treaties. He declared illegal most of the state fishing laws affecting Indians and ruled that the tribes should be given the opportunity to take up to 50 percent of the harvestable fish at their usual grounds. The state balked at enforcing his decision, and the issue dragged on for five more years until the United States Supreme Court upheld Boldt. But this delay did nothing to dim the accomplishment of the Indians whose courage and tenacity had helped pave the way for a new era of self-determination. ◀▦▶

ARCHITECTURE BASED ON TRADITION

From the tipis that stood in circles on the Plains to the sturdy plank houses that lined the Northwest coast, American Indian architecture was a product of the land and the people. Structures were built out of materials at hand—timber, reeds, earth, bark, brush, or animal hides— and reflected the people's lifeways: their religion, social organization, and methods of subsistence.

For a number of tribes, dwellings were sacred structures built in a way prescribed in visions or by deities. The fire that burned in the central hearth not only warmed and comforted the family but also served as a conduit for prayers. Sometimes the Indian home was a model of the universe itself, where everyone had a place and knew their role. The Lakota, for example, believed that the floor of their buffalo-hide tipi symbolized the earth, the sides the sky, and the poles the trails to the spirit world. A man's place was on the north side, a woman's on the south.

With the arrival of the Europeans, however, the Indian way of living began to erode, and in many places, it all but disappeared. As tribes were forced onto reservations, often in harsh climates and unfamiliar locations, tipis, wigwams, chickees, hogans, longhouses, wickiups, and earth lodges rich in spirituality gave way to the white man's log cabin.

Beginning in the 1970s, many Native American communities began searching for modern building styles that would reflect their values and provide a sense of community and continuity similar to that offered by their traditional structures. Architects, some of whom were Indians themselves, began borrowing from traditional designs, cultural elements, and age-old symbols. Among the first buildings to incorporate the essence of tribal life were museums. The Indian Pueblo Cultural Center in Albuquerque, New Mexico, patterned after the stone and adobe pueblo at Chaco Canyon, paved the way for other projects.

Architects who are tasked with designing buildings for Indians have discovered that consultation with the people is an essential part of the process. "When any decision is being made, it is the Indian way to come together as a community and voice opinions for other tribal members to hear," explained Dennis Sun Rhodes, an Arapaho architect.

Before completing the design for The Museum at Warm Springs (Reservation) in Oregon, shown at right, the architects set up an office on the reservation and opened their doors to the community. "One crucial thing we got from those sessions," recalled one non-Indian architect, "was an understanding of the great importance tribal members placed on using authentic materials, materials that reflected their values and close ties to the land." As a result, local rock and timber were used in the construction. One of the designers of the Lakota Studies building at Sinte Gleska College in Rosebud, South Dakota, has described the process as "adapting to new circumstances and adopting new ways, yet staying true to the instructions given to the Lakota."

The design of The Museum at Warm Springs (Reservation) in Oregon (below) drew inspiration from the tipi, the universally recognized American Indian home, shown above in a Piegan Blackfeet encampment in 1900. The tipi's conical shape was one of the traditional forms borrowed from the three peoples that live on the reservation—the Northern Paiute, the Wasco, and the Warm Springs. The design on the museum wall is from a basket-weave pattern. The Indians built the museum to house tribal artifacts they had purchased in an effort to prevent their heirlooms from being bought up by collectors.

BUILDING A HEALING PLACE

The willow frame of a traditional sweat lodge (above), a steam bath used by many tribes for physical and spiritual purification, provided the model for the entrance to the Indian Health Service Hospital at Crow Agency, Montana (below). The hospital serves the Crow and Northern Cheyenne communities. Like the sweat lodge, the entrance of the hospital faces east, as do most of the patients' rooms. On the foyer wall is Northern Cheyenne artist Christopher Rowland's 31-foot mural, entitled "Healing Lodge" (top right), depicting a warrior carrying robes used to cover a sweat lodge frame. The foyer floor (bottom right) is adorned by a morning star design, symbol of the Northern Cheyenne. The building's exterior brickwork features Crow beadwork patterns.

INTIMATIONS OF AGE-OLD FORMS

The Ned Hatathli Cultural Center at the Navajo Community College in Tsaile, Arizona (below), was designed in the shape of a hogan (above), the traditional Navajo home. Constructed in the way Talking God made the original dwelling for First Man and First Woman, hogans face east to greet the rising sun. The six-story building is made of glass that reflects the surrounding landscape and sky. It houses a museum and art gallery as well as classrooms and administrative offices. The campus and most of the buildings are built in a similar style, signifying the importance of the hogan to the Navajo.

The Iroquois Indian Museum in Howes Cave, New York, is designed after the longhouse (above), symbol of the original Iroquois League of Five Nations. The longhouse expressed the Iroquois notion of community, of families living peacefully side by side under one curved roof. The museum houses an archaeological collection, a children's museum, and a gallery for contemporary Iroquois artists. Traditional elements incorporated into the design include a skylight reminiscent of the smoke holes that let sunlight into the longhouses, and cedar shingles that resemble the original elm-bark siding.

THE FLAVOR OF THE NORTHWEST

The floor plan (below, left) of a four-story building housing a museum of local Indian artifacts in Seattle, Washington, is patterned after a copper, a shieldlike piece of engraved copper that was a symbol of wealth to the people of the Northwest Coast. In the 1894 photograph above, a Kwakiutl is shown displaying a copper. Built on Lake Union, the building sits perpendicular to the shore with its main entrance facing the water, as did traditional Northwest plank houses.

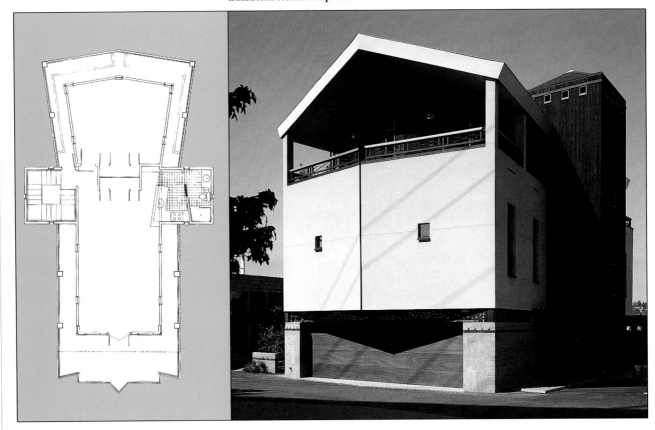

Reflecting the Haida plank house shown in the archival photograph above, totem figures carved on a pole topped by the fin of a dogfish (below, left) guard the glass-fronted, cedar-beamed council office of the Haida Indians in Skidegate, British Columbia. Following the practice of excavating the central area of a plank house for cooking and ritual use, the interior of the office is sunken. A skylight overhead represents a smoke hole.

3

IN PURSUIT OF SOVEREIGNTY

A San Juan Pueblo boy wears the regalia of a Plains warrior for the Comanche Dance, a celebration of a long-ago victory over Comanche raiders. The dance, purely social in nature, is often held during the religious feast days of the Eastern Pueblo peoples.

"What have we done?" Charles Lohah asked LaDonna Harris as they walked across a Washington, D.C., parking lot in the middle of an unseasonably cool September evening in 1975. After much debate, Lohah and Harris and the other representatives of 22 tribes had just agreed to form a new organization to help reservations rich in energy resources maximize profits for their own people. Optimistic about the possibilities for such a federation but concerned about potential pitfalls, Lohah, an Osage then with the Native American Rights Fund, asked Harris, a Comanche who headed Americans for Indian Opportunity, "Is this turkey gonna fly?"

More than a few Indians doubted that the organization—dubbed the Council of Energy Resource Tribes (CERT)—would ever get off the ground. Skeptics recalled that great Indian leaders of the past, such as the mid-18th-century Ottawa war chief Pontiac and the early-19th-century Shawnee war chief Tecumseh, had forged successful short-lived alliances, but that long-term multitribal efforts had historically faltered. And with good reason. North America's many diverse tribes had different needs. And even in the late 20th century, the idea of one coalition speaking for its many parts seemed highly problematic. In addition, many communities were split between pro-development Indians interested in exploiting their natural resources in order to bring jobs and money to reservations and anti-development Indians bent on preserving tribal lands in a pristine state. Infused with a strong attachment to the earth, these Indians mourned the losses already caused by previous resource extractions. They shared the 2ments of an 83-year-old Navajo woman who, having seen the adverse effects of strip mining, angrily asked, "How can we give something of value to Mother Earth to repay the damages done to her?"

Nonetheless, CERT forged ahead with its charter "to promote the general welfare of energy resource-owning tribes and their people through the protection, conservation, and prudent management of their oil, natural gas, coal, uranium, geothermal, and oil shale resources." Ironically, many reservation lands once thought to be useless had often proved oth-

erwise. According to 1977 Department of the Interior estimates, 34 tribes owned 11 percent of all coal nationwide, including nearly one-third of the low-sulfur, surface-minable coal west of the Mississippi River; 40 to 50 percent of all privately held uranium; four percent of America's oil and natural gas reserves; and substantial amounts of oil shale and geothermal power.

The timing for the creation of CERT was auspicious. An oil embargo begun in the fall of 1973 by the Organization of Petroleum Exporting Countries (OPEC) after the outbreak of the Arab-Israeli War had caused gasoline prices to soar and created long lines of cars at gas stations all across America. With the country in the grip of an unprecedented energy crisis and searching for alternative fuels, many western tribes believed

that their land's resources held the answer to both the nation's energy shortage and their own economic woes. Large corporations had been exploiting coal and other minerals on Indian lands for decades. The Indians favored reevaluating those old, outdated agreements in favor of new contracts that would treat them more fairly.

Previously, all tribal contracts with energy corporations had been negotiated by the Bureau of Indian Affairs. In the years leading up to the formation of CERT, many tribes realized that these contracts were seriously flawed. The Navajo and the Hopi, for example, belatedly discovered the deleterious effects of the 1966 agreement they had signed with Peabody Western Coal Company allowing for strip mining in the sacred Black Mesa area. In addition to environmental losses, the Indians had suffered staggering financial losses over the years because they had agreed to coal leases that paid flat-rate royalties rather than a percentage of the market value of the coal mined. Long-term contracts drawn up before the energy crisis meant that some tribes were receiving less than $.15 per ton of coal even though the market rate in the early 1970s had risen to $17.00 a ton. LaDonna Harris and her Americans for Indian Opportunity organization

Perched on a platform in northeastern Alaska, a Gwich'in lookout (right) watches for the first sign of the migrating Porcupine caribou herd (above). The Gwich'in are fighting against proposed oil exploration in the Arctic National Wildlife Refuge, the 1.5-million-acre coastal plain that is the calving ground for the 180,000-head herd.

conducted a study of several of the business agreements and concluded that "in the whole world, there
were no contracts as bad as the tribes' leases."

CERT began quietly, working as a service organization to advise its members about negotiations with
companies and to provide a clearinghouse of information about energy resources. Tribes wanted to negoti-
ate their own leases without interference from the Bureau of Indian Affairs, but most of them lacked the
economic and technical expertise to do so. Backed by
federal grants, CERT provided outside assistance from
legal and scientific experts who helped tribes renegoti-
ate more favorable leases to ensure better royalties and hiring clauses that
guaranteed a percentage of energy-related jobs to reservation residents.
There had been few such jobs available. In 1975, for example, when CERT
was founded and fuel prices reached an all-time peak on the Navajo Reser-

A Gwich'in girl dressed in caribou-skin clothing and holding a drum bearing the likeness of a caribou (top left); the rack of caribou ribs roasting (bottom left); and the beautifully decorated caribou-hide altar cloth (above) attest to the material and spiritual bonds between the Gwich'in, or "caribou people," and their namesake animal.

vation, energy resource development provided jobs for less than five percent of the Navajo labor force, and 67 percent of the Navajo adult population remained underemployed or without a job altogether.

CERT members also lobbied for agreements that gave Native Americans a greater voice in the development of their tribal lands. As Dewitt Dillon, Crow business manager of the coal-rich Crow Indian Reservation in southern Montana, explained: "We are looking for leases that will give the tribe control over development. We don't intend to impede progress, but we do want the natural resources to be developed in a way compatible with the tribe's environment. We are determined to shape our own destiny."

The organization maintained a low profile for a time, but then suddenly it was thrust into the spotlight. When CERT chairman Peter MacDonald compared the organization to OPEC in 1977, this little-known advisory group suddenly made national headlines. It was a public relations nightmare for the Indians. Speaking in Phoenix, Arizona, the colorful MacDonald, who was also Navajo tribal chairman, insisted that tribes had suffered from the same poor social conditions and resource exploitation that plagued many OPEC nations. The news media focused not on the similarities in living conditions on Indian reservations and in Third World oil-exporting countries that in fact existed, but on MacDonald's hint that the tribes might stage their own embargo if they failed to receive necessary federal funding. "We ask now quietly and constructively. We will not ask much longer," he warned. "We will withhold future growth at any sacrifice if that is necessary to survival."

Media coverage of MacDonald's remarks resulted in a backlash against CERT. News reporters across the nation began portraying Native Americans as unpatriotic and vastly wealthy—the equivalents of Arab and Iranian oil sheiks who would not think twice about holding up America for outrageous sums of money. The impressions of widespread Indian affluence were grossly misleading—the 1980 census found that 40 percent of Indians on reservations still lived below the poverty level, compared with

12 percent of the nation as a whole. Even among CERT members, only two reservations—the Jicarilla Apache in New Mexico and the Osage in Oklahoma—had incomes above $10,000 per capita per year. A high ratio of population to energy resources meant that the Navajo, by contrast, had an average income of only $900 per year.

Concerned about the bad press and worried that CERT no longer represented their best interests, the Cheyenne River Sioux in South Dakota and the Wind River Shoshone and Arapaho in Wyoming resigned from the organization. Other Indian critics alleged that because CERT received funding from the Department of Energy it was more interested in promoting energy development than in resource management. By 1983 CERT had overspent its budget and was forced to close its Washington, D.C., offices and lay off most of its work force. The organization lost further influence as the price of energy came down in the 1980s. Based in Denver, CERT still exists, but now it focuses primarily on providing technical assistance rather than on lobbying for political change or speaking out on behalf of member tribes. A 1985 government task force reported that only 14 percent of Indians lived on reservations that annually earned oil or coal revenues equal to $500 or more per resident. It was clear that reports of an "American Middle East" springing up on the reservations had been greatly exaggerated.

CERT's vexed history stands as but one short chapter in the long story of the efforts of North American tribes to free themselves from both poverty

An Arapaho technician (above) checks the water temperature below a dam on the Wind River Indian Reservation in Wyoming. His people and their former enemies, the Shoshone, have shared the reservation since 1878. Today both tribes work together to protect their water rights. In the photograph at right, a Shoshone medicine man wades in the still pristine waters of the Little Wind River, a Wind River tributary.

and federal assistance programs, as well as the bureaucracy and dependency that often accompany them. Although not as colorful as the confrontational activism of the 1960s and early 1970s, the history of Native American politics in the late 20th century has nonetheless been marked by gains of enduring value. These gains, however, have been hard-won and often controversial. Indians continue to debate the proper use of water resources, tribal land management, and economic opportunities: Some tribal members insist that survival depends on the degree to which Indians can exploit the opportunities offered by American society at large, while others reject that society, contending that survival depends on preserving and reconstructing their own culture. Groups continue to confront the question: What is a tribe? "Is it a traditionally organized band of Indians following customs with medicine men and chief dominating the policies?" asks the noted Sioux writer and lawyer Vine Deloria Jr., "or is it a modern corporate structure attempting to compromise with modern white culture?"

In the case of CERT, the protest arena shifted from Red Power demonstrations to corporate boardrooms. The halls of Congress have provided another forum for change where Native Americans have achieved noteworthy legislative victories over the last 20 years. In addition, American Indian groups have fought numerous courtroom battles involving land claims, resource rights, and tribal sovereignty disputes. Economic development has also raised the standard of living for several tribes, but by no means all. Along with these steps toward self-determination has come a cultural reawakening. Although their ancestors were encouraged to assimilate, many of today's Indians celebrate and declare a unique heritage that places them apart from mainstream America. The increased educational opportunities of the previous generation prepared a new cadre of Indian lawyers, teachers, doctors, artists, politicians, businesspeople, and other professionals who have worked to ensure that Indian communities continue not only to survive but also, in many cases, to thrive.

The battles, however, are far from over. In spite of legal and legislative victories, many Native American communities continue to suffer from an alarmingly poor quality of life. For every tribe earning a profit from energy resources, there are hundreds of Indian households without electricity, running water, or indoor plumbing. A series of federal budget cuts in the 1980s virtually crippled some reservation economies and resulted in the loss of badly needed medical and municipal services. Unemployment hovers as high as 80 percent in some communities. Inadequate medical facilities are unable to cope with serious health problems; infant mortality rates remain among the highest in the nation. Poor social conditions and a lack of jobs lead to inevitable frustration as well as to crime, vandalism, domestic abuse, and perhaps most insidious, widespread alcoholism.

Navajos have exchanged jewelry or crafts for money and supplies at the Carson Trading Post (top right) in Farmington, New Mexico, since the early 1920s. Florence King, a Yanktonai Sioux woman (bottom right), sells her handmade star quilts, beaded cradleboards, and other handiwork from her home on the Fort Peck Indian Reservation in northeastern Montana.

Such painful struggles have made it clear to Indians that they must find new ways of coping with life within the larger American nation. Many have recognized that the failures of previous government-tribal relations have stemmed largely from the fact that the United States government, not the tribal community, has determined Indian destiny and defined Indian needs. Whether they have been well intentioned or exploitative, the efforts of outsiders to solve the Indian "problem" have failed repeatedly. Many Native Americans perceive the efforts of government agencies, such as the Bureau of Indian Affairs, as impediments to progress and autonomy because they perpetuate non-Indian control over tribal affairs.

Perhaps more than any other modern president, Richard M. Nixon sympathized with the Indian desire to achieve a balance between retaining federal support and establishing true sovereignty. During his years in office, Nixon sought to establish a middle ground. The goal, he said, was to "strengthen the Indian's sense of autonomy without threatening his sense of community." Other politicians followed Nixon's lead. In 1974 Congress passed the Indian Financing Act, which established a revolving loan fund to encourage economic development on reservations. In addition, the federal government committed itself to provide Indians with subsidies

Nearing the end of a five-month, cross-country trek to draw attention to the plight of many Native Americans, participants in the Longest Walk arrive in Washington, D.C., on July 15, 1978 (above). The Indians set up a tipi and staged demonstrations against anti-Indian legislation in view of the White House (above, right).

and business grants, and authorized some federal agencies to place special emphasis on Indian economic needs. The following year, the Indian Self-Determination and Educational Assistance Act, a bill sponsored by Senator Henry Jackson of the state of Washington, became law. This landmark piece of legislation directed the Bureau of Indian Affairs and the Indian Health Service to draw up agreements with tribes interested in providing programs and services previously administered by those agencies. In addition, the Indian Health Care Improvement Act of 1976 provided more government funding for these programs and established classes to train healthcare professionals for work in Indian communities. And the Indian Child Welfare Act addressed the widespread problem of Indian children being adopted by non-Indian parents. In the interest of promoting the "stability and security of Indian tribes and families," this legislation decreed that many Indian adoption cases should be heard in tribal courts. It also established a series of guidelines for cases heard in state courts dictating that preference be given to Indian guardians.

Also of major political significance was the creation in 1975 of the American Indian Policy Review Commission, formed to study the "historical and legal developments underlying the Indian's unique relationship with the federal government in order to determine the nature of and scope of necessary revisions in the formulation of policies and programs for the

benefit of Indians." For two years, the commission, composed of five Indians and legislators from areas with large Indian populations, toured the country and conducted extensive hearings. Their final report contained 206 recommendations and strongly emphasized the importance of allowing for tribal sovereignty while still maintaining a trust relationship with the United States government. The tribe's "sovereign rights," the report stressed, "are of the highest legal standing, established through solemn treaties, and by layers of legislative actions." In summary, the commission concluded that Indian nations should exercise the same judicial and legal powers as states and territories, including the power to pass and enforce laws and receive government funds. Such findings seemed to be too extreme to Representative Lloyd Meeds (D-Wash), who served as vice chair of the committee. He disagreed strongly with the majority definition of tribalism and sovereignty. This minority dissent proved damaging; many of the commission's recommendations for an overhaul of federal policy were ignored. It was clear, however, that tribes had made significant legislative gains during the 1970s.

The federal court system proved to be the Indian community's best hope for enforcing and upholding these new legislative gains. "On the whole," noted Vine Deloria Jr., "the [Supreme] Court has been a friend, not a foe, and the last bastion of sympathetic understanding in the American political system available to the tribes." A dramatic increase in opportunities for Indians to pursue college and graduate degrees produced several hundred Indian lawyers by the 1970s. Backed by the Native American Rights Fund, created in 1971, or by tribal treasuries, attorneys worked aggressively on behalf of individual and tribal clients to make new and existing laws work for them and to ensure that historical treaties were upheld. The Supreme Court became final arbiter on numerous Indian rights issues during this period, ruling on no fewer than 35 Indian law cases in the 1970s.

One of the greatest victories came in the mid-1970s when the 3,000 members of the Passamaquoddy and Penobscot tribes recovered "aborig-

inal title" to almost two-thirds of the state of Maine. The tribes pressed their case based on the all-but-forgotten Indian Trade and Intercourse Act of 1790 that regulated trade between whites and Indians and established a trust relationship between the tribes and the federal government. An out-of-court settlement led to the 1980 Maine Indian Claims Settlement Act, which awarded each tribe $40.3 million in exchange for more than 12 million acres in Maine. Rather than distributing the award among tribal members, however, both groups invested for long-term gain.

One-third of the money went toward buying 300,000 acres of land. Another third went into conservative investments whose proceeds are divided among tribal members annually. The final portion was invested directly in business ventures through the newly formed Tribal Assets Management Company. Both groups hoped to find investment opportunities that paid off in economic dividends as well as in long-term social and employment opportunities for their communities.

It was through these business ventures that the fortunes of the groups diverged. The Penobscot investments in a reservation ice hockey arena and an audio- and videocassette manufacturing business failed to make money. The Passamaquoddies, by contrast, bought Maine's third-largest blueberry farm and made up their initial investment within two years. In addition, they bought two radio stations and, in 1983, the only cement plant in New England. When they sold the plant five years later, they earned an estimated profit of $60 million.

Although few tribes have seen economic benefits equal to the Pas-

Bill Denny holds a certificate from the state of Montana granting the Rocky Boy's Native American Church permission to use peyote in its worship services. Denny, a major force in bringing Peyotism to Rocky Boy's, learned the rituals from the Crow in the early 1930s.

samaquoddies', other groups have also won key legal victories by reexamining old agreements. In 1979 the federal courts upheld an earlier ruling granting 25 tribes of coastal Washington State special rights to fish for salmon and trout in Puget Sound. In Wisconsin, the courts determined that a 19th-century treaty guaranteed Ojibwa spear fishermen special privileges, much to the dismay of sport fishermen and local government officials. And the Quechan tribes who live along the California-Arizona border gained the right to expand their reservation to boundaries agreed upon in an 1884 contract. The Supreme Court has also repeatedly upheld the economic rights of tribes as sovereign nations, striking down state efforts to tax reservation property or the income of reservation Indians and business.

One of the most famous battles involves the Lakota Sioux, who have been fighting since 1920 to reclaim ownership of the Black Hills of South Dakota. When the case finally reached the Supreme Court in 1979, the justices awarded the Lakota $105 million in compensation for the land seized in 1877 after gold was discovered there. But the Lakota want their land back. They have repeatedly refused the money, leaving it instead in the federal treasury, where it sits collecting interest.

Landmark legal and legislative victories as well as the initial success of the Council of Energy Resource Tribes and the strong recommendations of the American Indian Policy Review Commission were not without consequences—although some were negative. During the latter half of the 1970s, in fact, a backlash developed against Indians and Indian interests in the United States.

A crescent formed from earth—called the half-moon altar—is the focal point of the peyote ceremony. A fire of cedar shavings inside the half-moon produces an aromatic smoke through which the ritual paraphernalia are passed in order to become purified. The hand-rolled cigarettes are tobacco offerings placed at the moon's directional points.

Small anti-Indian groups formed around reservations and eventually organized into the national Interstate Congress for Equal Rights and Responsibilities, which lobbied to abolish preferential treatment granted to Indians and other minori-

ties. Newspapers and periodicals published editorials denouncing the special government status afforded to tribes under headlines such as "Goodies for Minorities" and "Too Obsessed with Minorities." In northern Wisconsin, threatening bumper stickers declaring "Save a Fish—Spear an Indian" appeared in response to a battle over Ojibwa fishing rights. Members of Congress also participated in the backlash by introducing bills such as the Indian Equal Opportunity Act of 1977, which proposed abrogating all treaties between the United States and individual tribes, abolishing the trust relationship, and abandoning the reservations.

On February 11, 1978, a large group of Indians, led by the Sioux Ernie Peters, met in San Francisco to begin a 3,000-mile transcontinental trek called the Longest Walk. The event was intended not only to protest the detrimental legislative bills, but also, as the name implied, to commemorate the forced removal of numerous tribes in the 1800s. By the time the group reached Washington, D.C., on July 15, their numbers had swelled to about 1,500 Indians and non-Indians, who gathered at the Washington Monument grounds for a rally. Their rhetoric was fiery and punctuated by the beat of traditional drums. Richard Mohawk, an AIM member from California, encouraged the cheering crowd, which included blacks, whites, and a group of Buddhist monks as well as Indians, to work in solidarity with what he called the oppressed populations of the world: "The people of Cuba and Vietnam rose up and threw off imperialism, and that's

A member of Rocky Boy's Native American Church shovels hot rocks into a sweat lodge where worshipers often ritually cleanse themselves before a peyote meeting. Customarily held on a Saturday night and lasting until dawn, the meetings consist of singing, praying, and ingesting peyote buttons or peyote tea.

going to happen here. The Palestinians, the PLO, they are indigenous people, they are warriors. We must extend our hand. It is only a matter of time that all indigenous people stand up and shake off the yoke of imperialism."

Although the language was combative, the mood was peaceful. The stated goal of the walk was to raise public consciousness through educational and religious means in an effort to defeat the "anti-Indian" proposals before Congress. As Clyde Bellecourt, a walk leader and AIM founder, explained: "We are here to let America know that everything hasn't been stolen from us, that we are still a way of life that survives. We are here to stop one of the most massive, criminal assaults ever to take place against our people." In fact, none of the backlash bills had any real chance of passing Congress. At least one activist acknowledged this at the rally, but he insisted that the walk was nonetheless necessary.

Indians have also felt the impact of a cultural backlash on the judicial level. In 1978 the Supreme Court decided in a case concerning the Suquamish tribe that Indian courts have no jurisdiction over non-Indian

A little girl helps serve the feast that the peyote meeting's sponsor has provided for the participants. The feast normally takes place several hours after sunrise, when the roadman ended the ceremony by singing the Quitting Song.

BEARING WITNESS TO A MIRACLE

In August 1994, a farm in Janesville, Wisconsin, stocked with an exotic assortment of peacocks, llamas, rabbits, foxes, and buffalo was transformed overnight into a place of pilgrimage for scores of Native Americans. They came to marvel at a creature they regarded as the living embodiment of the sacred White Buffalo Calf Woman of Plains Indian lore. Miracle, as the dark-eyed, light-haired calf was dubbed by the farmer on whose plot she was born, was indeed a prodigy—the first female white buffalo, other than an albino, encountered in the 20th century. The pilgrims believed that she had arrived as prophesied to usher in a new age of harmony.

According to legend, White Buffalo Calf Woman first appeared centuries ago in the guise of a beautiful maiden clad in radiant white buffalo hides. Two Lakota Sioux warriors were out hunting buffalo for their hungry people when they spotted her walking toward them across the plains. One of the two grasped her lustfully as she approached and was transformed into a pile of bone and ash. The other kept a reverent distance and earned her blessing. She asked him to return home and prepare a lodge for her arrival. The following day she appeared as promised, bringing with her as a gift a sacred pipe, whose smoke would ever after symbolize their new kinship and carry the prayers of the people to Wakan Tanka, or the Great Spirit. After promising to return one day, she departed in the form of a white buffalo calf.

In the late 1800s, the Lakota holy man Black Elk prophesied that White Buffalo Calf Woman would reappear in seven generations to restore tranquillity to a troubled world. For those who flocked to the farm in Janesville, Miracle was the fulfillment of that promise. In the words of Floyd Hand, a Lakota medicine man, her birth foretold unity "for all nations, black, red, yellow, and white."

The calf called Miracle sits placidly by her dark-haired mother in their pasture. The white calf's appearance "marks a new beginning," said Wayne McArthur, "and gives hope to our people."

Among the offerings to the white calf affixed to a tree by the buffalo pasture are medicine wheels, dream catchers, sweet grass, and eagle feathers. Such feathers were the most precious gift, explained Wayne McArthur, a Nakota Sioux who traveled here from Canada, because the "eagle flies closest to the Creator."

defendants, even when a non-Indian breaks the law on reservations. The greatest judicial defeats, however, came in a series of Supreme Court rulings on Indian religious freedom.

In 1978 Congress passed the American Indian Religious Freedom Act, which aimed to "protect and preserve for American Indians their inherent right of freedom to believe, express, and exercise [their] traditional religions, including but not limited to access to sites, use, and possession of sacred objects, and the freedom to worship through ceremonials and traditional rites." The act was designed to permit Indian use of federally protected wild animals and birds whose feathers or skins were essential to rituals, to allow for use of peyote—a hallucinogenic cactus—in sacred ceremonies, and to protect lands used for religious pilgrimages, vision quests, or burials.

While this represented a victory on paper, the act failed to live up to its promise and did not stand up to judicial challenges. For example, the courts have subsequently allowed an Arizona ski resort firm to develop the San Francisco Peaks, an area sacred to the Navajo and Hopi, and permitted the U.S. Forest Service to build a road through a range of mountains that play a central role in the spiritual life of the Yurok of northern California. A decision in 1988 curtailed the rights of certain Northwest Coast Indians to bury their dead on traditional sacred ground. In this case, the Supreme Court decided that while the Bill of Rights did protect religious practice, it did not protect a religious area, even if demolition of the area meant the religion could no longer be practiced.

Another emphatic defeat for Indian religious freedom was a ruling that came in 1990. The case concerned two Oregon men who were denied un-

Dressed mostly in traditional finery, six students from the Crow Poets Program in Pryor, Montana, stand with the program director at a banquet hosted by the community in their honor in 1994. Later that year, the young poets read selections from their works, which focus on the importance of preserving Crow lands and traditions, at the Library of Congress in Washington, D.C.

employment benefits after being fired from their jobs at a drug rehabilitation program because they had ingested peyote as part of a Native American Church ceremony. Peyote is essential in the church's ritual, and the federal government and 23 states permit it to be used for that purpose. Because Oregon law prohibits use of the cactus under any circumstances, the Court ruled that the First Amendment did not protect the men's right to religious freedom. In a strongly worded dissent to the controversial ruling, Justice Harry A. Blackmun accused the majority of a "wholesale overturning of settled law" on religious rights and compared the Indian's use of peyote to the sacramental use of wine in Christian ritual. Congress has since remedied this particular Supreme Court ruling. On October 7, 1994, President William J. Clinton signed into law a religious freedom bill that guaranteed the right of Native Americans to use peyote in traditional ceremonies.

While Indian lawyers and legislators have been fighting for sovereignty for Indian nations, a new generation of Native American artists has sought to define and depict contemporary Indian culture. Discontented with Hollywood's stereotypical portrayals of Indians as either brutal savages or romanticized children of nature, native writers have taken pen in hand to probe the essence of Indian life in modern times. While these authors recognize and often represent the despair that permeates their communities, they also see much to celebrate. Sparked by the Kiowa-Cherokee N. Scott Momaday's *House Made of Dawn,* which won the Pulitzer Prize in 1969, contemporary Indian writers have fueled a Native American renaissance. From the Athapaskan Mary Tallmountain, to the Creek Joy Harjo, to the Blackfeet-Gros Ventre James Welch, Indian writers across America have published works that have won critical acclaim and brought Indian people and their problems to a non-Indian audience.

These authors come face-to-face with the stark realities of Indian life in the late 20th century. Michael Dorris, who is of Modoc descent, explored the devastating effects of Indian alcoholism in his narrative *The Broken Cord,* which won the 1989 National Book Critics Circle Award. An account of his experience as the adoptive father of a boy with fetal alcohol syndrome, the book traces Dorris's journey to discover the roots of his son's illness as well as the implications of the disease for the entire Native American community. Dorris and others estimate that fetal alcohol syndrome and fetal alcohol effect rates among Native Americans are five to 25 times higher than those for other populations. He fears as many as 50 percent of the infants born in some Indian communities may eventually be affected if alcoholism continues to spread unchecked among women of childbearing age. Dorris also collaborates with his wife, Louise Erdrich. Of Turtle Mountain Ojibwa descent, Erdrich has won critical acclaim by observing reservation life through a fictional lens. Her 1994 novel *The Bingo Palace,* for example, offers a wry look at Indian gaming, played out when a wealthy reservation entrepreneur proposes building a federally sanctioned bingo hall on sacred Ojibwa ground.

Many writers also manage to mix modern-day realities with powerful ancient myths, resulting in works like Paula Gunn Allen's "Deer Woman." In this story, a traditional Pueblo legend of a woman transformed into a supernatural deer blends with details of modern city life. Indeed, the age-old art of storytelling has emerged as a central theme for many Indian poets and novelists. To repeat and adapt the oral tradition handed down from one's ancestors becomes an act of cultural survival, as potent in its own way as political protest, legislative reform, or courtroom battles. Leslie Marmon Silko, an author of mixed Laguna Pueblo, Mexican, and white ancestry, begins her 1981 collection *Storyteller* by remembering her Aunt Susie, who bequeathed to her a legacy of stories. Silko describes Laguna culture as an "entire vision of the world/which depended upon memory/and retelling by subsequent generations." Also included in the collection is the short story "Storyteller," which Silko has identified as one of her favorites. It centers on an Indian girl growing up in Alaska who comes to realize the power of narrative. Like Scheherazade in *The Arabian Nights' Entertainments,* she must tell a story—of her parents' death at the hands of unscrupulous white traders—in order to preserve her own life. Silko's poem "The Storyteller's Escape" echoes such a commitment to narration: "With these stories of ours/we can escape almost anything/With these stories we will survive."

One variety of traditional story that has proved particularly ripe for reinterpretation in modern literature is the trickster tale. Almost every tribe in North America has a legendary trickster: sometimes a coyote, a spider, a rabbit, a raven, or sometimes a human being. Called Nanapush by the Ojibwa and Iktomi by the Lakota, these characters are known for their tremendous energy and ability to change shape. In her award-winning 1984 *Love Medicine,* Louise Erdrich updates the traditional Ojibwa trickster to create Gerry Nanapush, a modern Indian who uses his shape-shifting skills to break out of the state prison. And the Ojibwa writer Gerald Vizenor creates Luster Browne, or Lusterbow, in his work

This 23-foot statue carved of red cedar by Nuuchanulth (Nootka) artist Joe David was displayed by the Indians of Vancouver Island, British Columbia, as part of a protest in 1984 against commercial logging on Meares Island, a 22,000-acre rain forest containing some of the oldest red cedars in Canada.

The Trickster of Liberty. Consigned to a supposedly worthless parcel of land by government bureaucrats, Lusterbow flourishes as the self-proclaimed "Baron of Patronia." He forms a union with Novena Mae Ironmoccasin, an orphan raised by Benedictine nuns; the two share a zesty love life and conceive 10 children.

The Sioux Philip J. Deloria accounts for the enduring popularity of such tales by suggesting that Indians themselves have existed in the 20th century as trickster peoples. Forced to adapt to American society, they have lived their lives as shape-shifters able to permeate boundaries between white America and reservations. "The Mohawk warriors hanging from New York skyscrapers, the Pueblo drummers at the Stock Exchange, the Indian volunteers in American wars, the Indian lawyer in court," he writes, "all of these people have understood, sometimes out of necessity, the trickster essence of cultural interaction and coexistence."

Native journalists across the United States and Canada have also realized the importance of telling their own stories. Frustrated by what many perceive as biased reporting by the television networks, major magazine publishers, and newspapers, they have worked for the opportunity to relay their own news. This desire has inspired the establishment of a number of Indian newspapers, such as *Wassaja Akwasasne Notes, News from Indian Country, The Lakota Times,* and the *Tundra Times,* which introduce readers to various tribal perspectives on current events. There are also more than two dozen Indian public radio stations, including the 50,000-watt Navajo station KTTN, and KILI, which serves 22,000 Lakota Sioux in southwestern South Dakota. Forgoing membership in the Washington-based National Public Radio and, along with it, such shows as "All Things Considered" and "Morning Edition" that form the mainstay of most public stations, KILI features local programming, including tribal news, a daily swap shop, high school sports reports, employment postings, blues and rap music, traditional Lakota chants, and song dedications for deceased relatives.

The station broadcasts in the Lakota language—a favorite feature for many listeners. "We're part of the revival of the Lakota Nation," explained Wilson Two Lance, the station's program director in 1995. "My mother

"Indian Country Today," a weekly newspaper published in Rapid City, South Dakota, carries news relevant to Indian people throughout the United States. Founded in 1980 as "The Lakota Times," the newspaper had a national circulation of nearly 19,000 copies by 1995.

A Lakota family jogs past the small building housing radio station KILI (above, left), the Voice of the Lakota Nation, on the Pine Ridge Reservation in South Dakota. In the photograph at left, a Lakota-speaking broadcaster entertains listeners with stories and relays community news.

came up when people would put kids in the deep freeze or wash their mouths out with soap if they spoke Lakota. Now my younger sisters can understand a little of the language." For more than a century, between 1886 and 1990 when the Native American Languages Act was passed, federal law prohibited the use of any Indian language in schools as part of the effort to promote assimilation. Today not only the Lakota but also the Cherokee, Creek, Choctaw, Chickasaw, Seminole, and other Indian nations are promoting language learning programs in an effort to preserve native voices. As the Ojibwa writer Gerald Vizenor explains, "The tribes were created in language" and preserving these languages is key to sovereignty for the tribes.

The story of KILI marks yet another chapter in the shift from the Indian activism of the sixties and early seventies to the quiet but diligent progress of the eighties and nineties. The station is in many ways a legacy of the 1973 Wounded Knee siege in which a few hundred Lakota Sioux and other Indian supporters took 11 hostages in protest against their own tribal government. When Ted Means, an AIM member and brother of activist Russell Means, was released from prison in 1979 after serving seven months for a rioting conviction (later overturned) that stemmed from the Wounded Knee incident, he joined forces with other AIM members to devise ways of improving communication on the reservation. Rejecting a television station or daily newspaper because of the prohibitively high cost, Means and fellow organizers settled on a radio station, which began broadcasting in 1983. "KILI is a shining example of self-determination," Means has said.

Indians elsewhere have created their own systems of higher education. When the Navajo Community College was established in 1968, it paved the way for a network of community colleges chartered and maintained by the tribes themselves. Late in the 1950s and early in the 1960s, the Navajo realized that their students were dropping out of colleges and returning to the reservation at an alarming rate; there was a 50 percent dropout rate after the freshman year alone. Many students were unable to deal with the staggering cultural differences they faced upon their arrival at school—and colleges and universities were unequipped to help them adjust. In response, members of the Navajo tribal council galvanized support for a tribally controlled community college that would offer a sound academic base for those wishing to continue their education, provide vocational and technical training, and serve as a center for the study and development of Navajo culture. In 1969 the college, housed in classrooms in a local boarding school, offered its first semester of classes to 309 students. Today it is one of the most successful tribal colleges in the country, with a main campus in Tsaile, Arizona, six smaller campuses, and a total enrollment of more than 2,000 students. Several other Indian communities, including the Oglala and Standing Rock Sioux and the Turtle Mountain Ojibwa, created their own community colleges with goals and curriculum tailored to their needs. In the mid-1990s, 29 tribal colleges enrolled almost 14,000 Indians on or near reservations across the United States.

While the federal government has continued to back the principles of self-determination and tribal sovereignty, tribes have seen drastic cutbacks in government funds and programs. In 1983 Indian aid was cut by more than one-third, from $3.5 billion to $2 billion. The consequences on reservations were disastrous. The Intertribal Alcoholism Treatment Center in Montana lost half of its counselors and most of its beds. In addition, Indians suffered as funds were cut for programs designed to serve the general population. When the Comprehensive Employment and Training Act was canceled, the Ponca in Oklahoma lost some 200 jobs. Cuts in Medicaid, food stamps, Head Start, and Aid to Families with Dependent Children have also affected many Indian families. "Just when we were starting to get our hands on the ledge, to pull ourselves up—whack! We're dropped right back where we were before," complained William Morgan, the director of administration and finance for the Navajo Nation, whose unemployment rate skyrocketed in the early 1980s.

Poverty will probably also continue to shape life for the 16,000 residents of Pine Ridge, the Oglala Sioux reservation in the Badlands of southwestern South Dakota. Shannon County, which stretches across most of the reservation, is the poorest in the nation. Tribal authorities estimate that in the early 1990s the unemployment rate here ran as high as 87 percent, with most jobholders working for a government agency. Alcoholism continues to take its deadly toll, and infant mortality and suicide rates are among the highest in the nation.

Reservation residents across the country continue to struggle against overwhelming obstacles. The 1990 census reported that Native Americans are the nation's most indigent group; 51 percent live below the poverty level. The average annual income for Indians on reservations is

Germaine DuMontier shows how to scrape hair from a deer hide in a native studies class at Salish Kootenai College on the Flathead Reservation in Pablo, Montana (top). Afterward, her students stretch the cleaned skin (bottom). Native studies classes are held on many reservations to help the younger generation master traditional crafts and skills.

less than $5,000. Health statistics are just as disheartening. In 1992 physicians at the University of Minnesota published a study of Indian youth in dozens of states, which determined that one in four Indian males had developed a drinking problem by the 12th grade. By the end of high school, one out of five girls and one out of eight boys have attempted suicide. "This is the most devastated group of adolescents in the United States," concluded one of the authors of the study.

Despite the bleak statistics, the Oglala and other communities persevere. The fissures that divided the Pine Ridge community during the Wounded Knee affair have begun to heal. AIM "warriors" and former Guardians of the Oglala Nation, supporters of the controversial former tribal president Richard Wilson, now work side by side on the tribal council. Still hampered by inadequate funds, Pine Ridge residents have nonetheless joined together to mend their community. A Lakota Fund has been created to invest in small businesses, such as video rental stores, auto body shops, and traditional craft vendors. "We don't have time for conflict between ourselves anymore," insisted Mona Wilson, director of an alcoholism recovery program in Pine Ridge in 1992. "We have too big a job to do in saving ourselves."

Alcoholism remains a grave problem. Some reservations are dotted with roadside markers at spots where drunk drivers have crashed and died, killing or injuring others in their path. Local Indians have dubbed the road to Pine Ridge "Killer Highway" because of the number of alcohol-related deaths that occur there. Pregnant mothers continue to give birth to infants irrevocably damaged by fetal alcohol syndrome and fetal alcohol effect.

Following the path of ancestors like the Hopi man pictured at left in 1910, Hopi youngsters in Keams Canyon, Arizona, begin a five-kilometer fun run sponsored by Wings of America, a Native American organization based in New Mexico. Central to the ritual lives of numerous tribes, running has become a popular means of promoting cultural identity, good health, and self-esteem among Indians everywhere.

The Oglala tribal council has declared a reservation-wide war on alcoholism. Members have responded not with standard support programs like Alcoholics Anonymous but rather with more culturally appropriate solutions. "Traditional approaches like Alcoholics Anonymous don't work here," explained Joe Lucero, an official at the Indian Health Service Hospital in Pine Ridge. With few telephones and no public transportation between homes on a reservation nearly the size of Connecticut, a recovering alcoholic finds it difficult to muster support during moments of temptation.

Rehabilitation sometimes involves traditional spirit medicine. Cecil Renville, a Sioux spiritual adviser, has effectively used the traditional sweat lodge purification rite in a therapy program for chemical dependency. Another weapon in the war against alcohol abuse is an organization called UNITY—United National Indian Tribal Youth. Founded in 1976 by a member of the Cherokee Nation, the group is designed to help Native American youth develop leadership skills and alternatives to destructive behavior.

The buzzword of the Reagan and later the Bush years was "economic development," centered on tribal initiative and profits. Although the consequences were disastrous for the residents of reservations like Pine Ridge, where resources were already inadequate, other Indian communities have managed to flourish. Slashing of the federal budget in the 1980s forced tribes to investigate other sources of revenue, social services, and administrative structures. Some tribes have imposed taxes on reservation property and sales, strengthened tribal jurisdiction over local driving violations and

criminal cases, and imposed Indian hiring-preference rules for reservation jobs. More than a dozen communities, including the Red Lake Ojibwa in Minnesota, the Menominee in Wisconsin, and the Absentee Shawnee and Kiowa in Oklahoma, have gained the right to introduce tribal license plates that feature the group's name and symbol on the plate. The tribes design and issue the plates, generate revenue from car registration fees, and arrange reciprocity agreements with states. These Indian-based solutions not only improve the reservation economy but also boost tribal pride.

One side effect of the rise in Indian autonomy has been the phenomenal growth of Indian gaming. Many tribes have taken advantage of their federal trust status to sidestep state gaming regulatory laws and open high-stakes bingo parlors and casinos. The rush began in 1979, when the Seminole won a court battle in Florida that denied the state the right to regulate bingo on reservations because of tribal sovereignty. The Supreme Court reaffirmed this decision in 1987, enabling the Mission Indians in California to continue with reservation bingo and card games because "state regulation would impermissibly infringe on tribal government." The 1988 Indian Gaming Regulatory Act permits tribes to offer high-stakes versions of whatever gambling is already allowed in a state (even if it is only allowed for charitable purposes, such as church bingo or charity roulette).

Since the passage of the Gaming Act, numerous tribes have established their own gaming ventures, including such large operations as the Choctaw's Silver Star Hotel Casino near Philadelphia, Mississippi, and the Shakopee Mdewakanton's (a Sioux group) Mystic Lake Casino in Minnesota.

A RICH TRADITION OF GAMING

Native Americans have always delighted in games of chance. Even though the proliferation of casinos in operation on a large number of today's reservations remains a source of controversy in some Indian communities—in general because of differences of opinion over strategies for long-term economic development—gambling has a long and rich tradition in Indian life.

Traditional Indian games, many of which are still played today, consist of two types: sleight-of-hand games, in which individual contestants or teams take turns attempting to guess where certain objects are hidden; and dice games, in which implements such as marked walnut shells, stones, peach pits, or acorns are thrown at random, frequently into a bowl or basket, or onto a hide mat.

Both types of games evolved from ancient ceremonies aimed at curing illnesses and promoting the reproduction of plants and animals. The games were originally played during the seasons of the year when the various communities of the tribe came together to renew social ties. Although the ceremonies may no longer exist, the games have survived as pastimes and amusements not only for players but for spectators as well, who often add to the excitement by chanting and playing drumming songs to encourage their favorites and distract their opponents.

An Oneida Indian deals cards for black-jack in the tribe's Turning Stone Casino near Syracuse, New York. In 1995, Indians owned and operated 124 casinos in 24 states. Many tribes use gaming revenues to support cultural revitalization programs.

In this 1890 photograph, Pueblo Indians play "patol," the Spanish name for an ancient stick-dice game derived from the Aztecs. How the sticks fall around a cobble placed inside a circle of stones determines the movements of a player's marker or "horse."

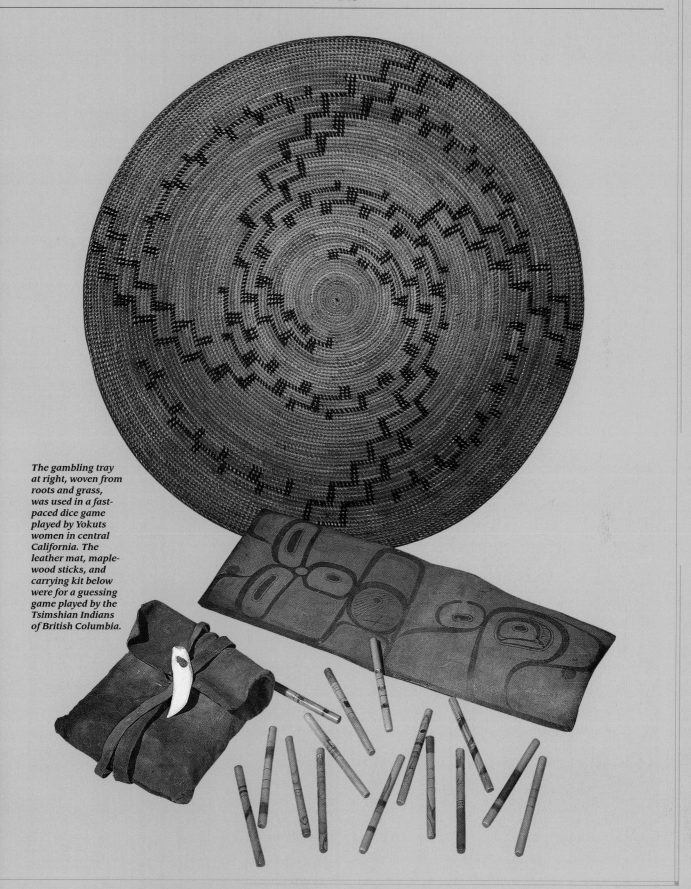

The gambling tray at right, woven from roots and grass, was used in a fast-paced dice game played by Yokuts women in central California. The leather mat, maple-wood sticks, and carrying kit below were for a guessing game played by the Tsimshian Indians of British Columbia.

SLEIGHT-OF-HAND CONTESTS

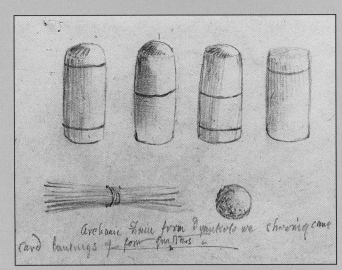

This sketch made in the 1880s by American ethnographer Frank Hamilton Cushing shows the pieces used in the Zuni hidden ball game—four wooden tubes, a stone ball, and a bundle of counting straws. The game was often played in the early spring to forecast the weather for the coming planting season.

As spectators from their communities sing songs of support, teams from Pryor (right) and Lodge Grass (left) compete in the 1987 Crow Hand Game championships at the Crow Indian Reservation in Montana. The teams take turns hiding and guessing the location of two elk teeth and two sticks, in a special order.

A modern hand game set crafted by Stephen Noyes, a Colville-Puyallup from Washington State's plateau region, consists of a buckskin bag, counting sticks, and four pieces of antler bone, two of them marked with bands. The object of the game is to guess which hand holds a marked bone.

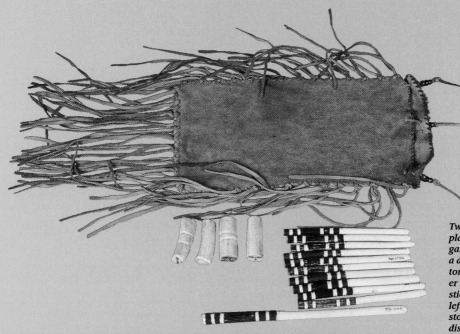

Two Ojibwa men play the moccasin game in 1920 before a drummer, a specta- tor, and a scorekeep- er holding counting sticks. The player at left displays four stones, one with a distinguishing mark, that he will try to slip under the moccasins on the blanket. His opponent in the bear-claw headdress will try to guess which moccasin hides which stone.

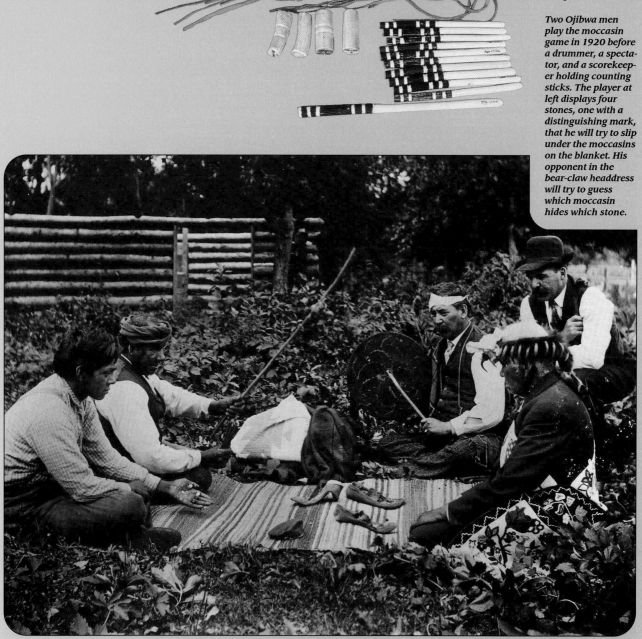

But the greatest gambling success story has been that of the Mashantucket Pequots in Connecticut. Their Foxwoods Casino, which at least one investment consultant has deemed the "most profitable casino in the world," reaped a gross yield of $800 million to $900 million in 1994. Annual profits are estimated at $400 million. Because the tribe is considered a sovereign body independent of the state, the Pequot pay no state taxes on their gambling income (except for a 25 percent tax on slot machines, which cannot otherwise be operated legally in Connecticut). Instead they direct the profits back to the tribe to provide housing for its members and support for health, education, cultural programs, and care for the elderly.

Stricter state controls, greater competition, and smaller customer bases have prevented other tribes from approaching the Pequot's annual income. But native groups continue to search for innovative ways of making gaming laws work for them. In what may be the boldest venture to date, the Coeur d'Alene tribe of northern Idaho is seeking to establish a weekly lottery, to be available in 36 states and the District of Columbia, in which participants can phone in their numbers and pay by credit card. Gaming manager David J. Matheson hopes the lottery will allow the 1,300 members of the tribe to "live a life of dignity and pride." At a March 1995

press conference, Matheson said: "There is no pride in the welfare line. Our people know what that feels like. We deserve something better. We want to pull ourselves back up by our bootstraps."

Not every Indian shares Matheson's enthusiasm for gambling. Ben Nighthorse Campbell, a Northern Cheyenne and U.S. senator from Colorado, insisted in a 1995 *New York Times* editorial that gambling is not the solution to the economic and social ills that pervade many reservations. "Media coverage of certain Indian gaming operations would have us believe Indians have struck gold and are not only rising out of their long history of impoverishment but getting rich quick," he wrote. "Nothing could be further from the truth." Campbell pointed out that, in spite of the phenomenal success of Foxwoods and a few other casinos, many gambling operations, such as that on the Fort Peck Reservation in northeastern Montana, have failed to bring wealth to local residents. Just as the relative prosperity of CERT members obscured the problems of many of the less-fortunate tribes, so likewise the success of gambling operations has masked some very real social ills that continue to plague the Indian population. Campbell insisted that hope for the future of all tribes lies in a diverse set of investments, from industry to tribal colleges.

Walking in solemn procession (left), descendants of Pretty Eagle, a late-19th-century Crow leader, carry the remains of their ancestor to his final resting place beneath a memorial tipi with war shield in the Bighorn Mountains of Montana (right). Pretty Eagle's bones were repatriated from the Smithsonian Institution in 1994.

REINVESTING IN A CULTURE

Although many Indian peoples have enjoyed a renaissance in the past few decades, none have experienced a more dramatic burst of prosperity than the Mashantucket Pequots of Connecticut. As recently as 1970, the Pequot—considered "rich and potent" by English colonists who settled in the area in the early 1600s—were perilously close to losing their identity. Their ancestors had suffered a murderous defeat at the hands of the English in 1637, and many of the survivors had been enslaved. Those Pequots who remained in the area, or returned there in later years, were afflicted by disease and poverty and victimized by prejudice.

By 1856 the reservation at Mashantucket had been pared down to barely 200 acres. By the 1960s, only two adult tribal members, Elizabeth George Plouffe and her half sister, Martha Langevin Ellal, still lived there. Determined to preserve a place for the Pequot, the women commanded their descendants to "hold on to the land."

Plouffe's grandson, Richard "Skip" Hayward, did just that—and more. Elected tribal chairman in 1975, he led successful battles to win federal recognition and reclaim reservation land. He urged other Pequots to join him in moving back to Mashantucket. In order to support their growing community, they opened a high-stakes bingo hall on the reservation in 1986. The operation quickly evolved into the nation's most lucrative casino. Most of the profits were plowed back into tribal housing, healthcare, and education.

The benefits have drawn hundreds of Pequots back to the reservation. Today, they are working to recover their past as well as to secure their future by conducting archaeological research, building a museum, and teaching the young about the culture of their ancestors.

Having reclaimed land wrested from them, the Mashantucket Pequots now occupy about 3,000 acres here in southeastern Connecticut.

Standing near the remnants of a 17th-century fortified Pequot settlement, museum director Theresa Bell reviews excavation plans with archaeologist Ross Harper.

Assistant museum director Charlene Jones and senior researcher Paul Costa examine a 17th-century document on microfilm in an effort to piece together the tribe's history, which will be preserved in the new Mashantucket Pequot Museum and Research Center.

An iron kettle hook, a clay pipe, and an unfinished metal knife are among the objects of native and European origin unearthed during the excavation of the fortified village, where Pequots traded with colonists.

INSPIRATION FROM NEAR AND AFAR

Little is known about Pequot traditions before the war of 1637, which disrupted the culture and nearly effaced the very word *Pequot*. The river that early colonists called the Pequot, for example, became known as the Thames. But recently Pequots have heightened their sense of cultural identity by drawing from their own oral tradition and by consulting with neighboring Algonquian tribes like the Narragansett and the Wampanoag. Ancient ceremonies are being revived. Classes in native crafts, song, and dance are offered for tribal elders and younger members alike at the reservation's new community center.

The Pequot are communing with Indians from other regions as well. Each September, the tribe hosts a four-day festival called Schemitzun, or the Feast of the Green Corn and Dance. Thousands of Indian dancers gather from all over North America, not simply to compete for big prize money but to give thanks for their blessings and join in a giant powwow that celebrates all that Native Americans hold in common.

Pequot singer Laughing Woman, accompanied by her husband Eagle Wings, performs at a celebration in October 1993 marking the groundbreaking for the museum and research center, which will be the largest facility of its kind owned and operated by Native Americans.

To bless the ground on which the museum will be built, Slow Turtle of the Wampanoag burns sage in a shell, dispersing the purifying smoke with the feather in his hand. Although the Pequot and neighboring groups have adopted some customs and traditions from Indians of other regions, many of their rituals have ancient roots in New England.

Pequot elders wear their traditional regalia in this 1995 photograph. The design of the hand-made attire was based on historical records of the clothing commonly worn by the Indians of southern New England in the early 17th century.

Four-year-old Jasmine Smith learns the Fancy Shawl Dance—which is popular among female powwow competitors from tribes around the country—at the recently constructed Pequot community center.

Beneath a sacred symbol made by youngsters at the child development center, five-year-old Clifford Sebastian works at a computer under the supervision of prekindergarten teacher Cathy Crippen. The center provides education, cultural activities, and day-care services for tribal youngsters.

The expansive museum and research center will feature a 200-foot tower symbolizing cultural resurgence and a semicircular "gathering space" evoking the fortified enclosures of early Pequot settlements. The complex will include, among other facilities, a 150,000-volume Native American research library, a children's library, a 300-seat theater, and an oral history center. Interactive videos and life-size dioramas will make history come alive for future generations of Pequots as well as for visitors to their community.

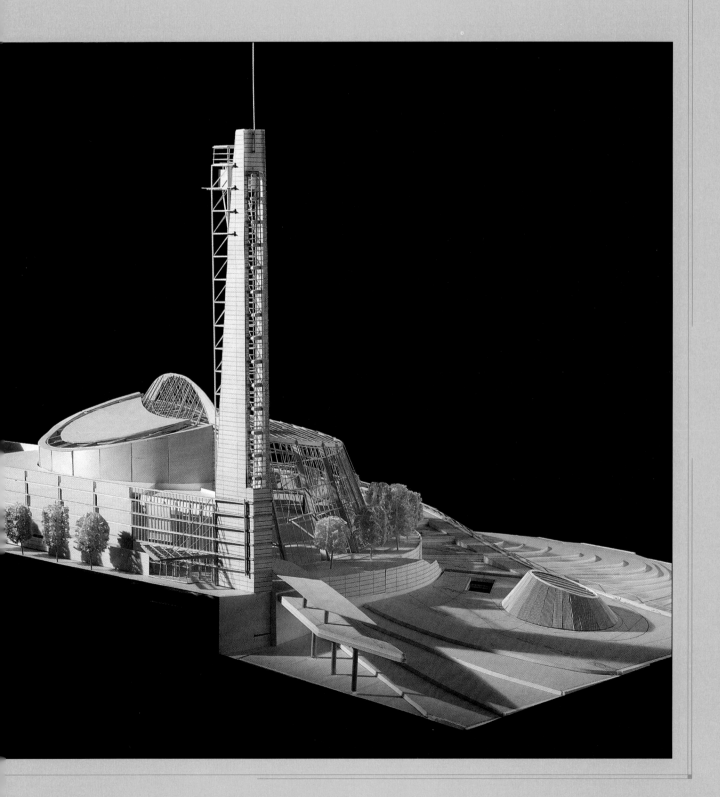

Other Native Americans fear that gaming may hasten the decline of traditional Indian values. "Many Indian nations look like Las Vegas," complained Onondaga artist and tribal council member Oren Lyons. "Why does Indian economic development have to revolve around gambling, bingo, and the sale of cigarettes and firecrackers? This kind of negative economic development results in 20 or 30 people fighting for a piece of the pie. It is based on quick profit with no concern for the effect it will have on Indian communities." Cecilia Mitchell, a Mohawk medicine woman who lives near the Saint Lawrence River in Canada, agreed with Lyons. "The sad part is that the people believe that if we don't have gambling, we don't have money, and there's no progress," she remarked. "We don't need that, because with gambling comes disruption of our lives. Therefore, inside their hearts, deep inside, they know it is dangerous. But they need money. They don't understand they don't need all that."

Dancers from many tribes enter the dance circle during the Grand Entry procession of a powwow at the Rocky Boy's Reservation in 1993. "It's an indescribable feeling when Grand Entry begins," one Assiniboin Jingle Dress Dancer said. "When I hear the song, drumbeat, bells, and war whoops, and see the bustles floating by, and the children's happy faces gleaming, my whole body tingles."

Festooned with colorful blankets and carrying a decorative tipi, a pickup truck at the 1992 Crow Fair in Crow Agency, Montana, proudly proclaims the heritage of its owner—a sentiment echoed by the license plate below.

Gambling is by no means the only successful business development project on reservations. The 8,000-member Mississippi Choctaw tribe, under the leadership of chief and savvy businessman Philip Martin, for example, manufactures greeting cards in addition to electrical appliances for Ford and General Motors, employing more than 3,000 individuals and boasting annual sales of more than $60 million. Today the tribe is one of the 10 largest employers in Mississippi.

Elsewhere, the Oglala Sioux and more than 30 other Great Plains tribes are trying to rebuild a buffalo-based economy with the help of the InterTribal Bison Cooperative, an organization created in 1992 to reintroduce buffalo to the region. The Indians hope that the new buffalo herds will not only bring a degree of economic security through the sale of their meat but also encourage a return of the traditional values and spiritual practices long associated with the animal.

In addition to their economic achievements, Native Americans could only be encouraged by signs in the last decades of the 20th century that the fires of cultural renewal continue to burn brightly. In 1989 Congress approved funding to the Smithsonian Institution for a new National Museum of the American Indian to be built by the year 2001 on the last available piece of ground on the Mall in Washington, D.C. Before the project could begin, the Smithsonian and various Indian groups negotiated the return of ancient artifacts—ceremonial and religious objects—which the Smithsonian had acquired. The Smithsonian also agreed to return human remains—Indian bones collected for the purposes of anthropological and anatomical study. Stanford University, meanwhile, had already begun repatriating the artifacts and remains it held. At a ceremony to rebury the bones returned to her family by Stanford, Rosemary Cambra, a California Indian, explained the importance of the move: "Our old ones gave life to us. Now we gave a final life to them by putting them to rest back where they belonged." In response to the outcry from the Indian community, Congress passed the 1990 Indian Graves Protection and Repatriation Act, which required all museums receiving fed-

eral funds to inventory their collections and return sacred objects to tribes.

Another outcome of Indian protest has been the Smithsonian's decision to solicit Indian input for the museum's buildings and displays. As a result, the new complex will focus on both living Indian cultures and traditional Indian history. As Oren Lyons, a member of the Onondaga Council of Chiefs, has explained to anthropologists and curators: "We will determine what our culture is. It has been pointed out that culture constantly changes. It is not the same today as it was a hundred years ago. We are still a vital, active Indian society. We are not going to be put in a museum or accept your interpretations of our culture."

The concerns of Lyons and others have been taken seriously, and the Native American community has played a central role in shaping the Smithsonian project. Douglas Cardinal, a Canadian architect of Native American ancestry, was chosen to design the main building on the Washington Mall. And W. Richard West, a Cheyenne-Arapaho lawyer, has been appointed chairman of the new museum. Other Native American involvement came in the form of a gift: $10 million from the Mashantucket Pequots, the largest donation ever given to the Smithsonian by a private source. Acknowledging that most tribes are unable to make such a magnanimous gesture, tribal chairman Richard "Skip" Hayward explained that "the name on the check will be the Mashantucket Pequot tribal nation, but in the broader sense, this is a gift on behalf of all Native Americans."

More than a century after they were deemed a vanishing people, American Indians refuse to disappear. According to the 1990 census, 1.9 million Americans classify themselves as either Indian, Eskimo, or Aleut—an increase of more than one-third over the 1980 estimate. Of that figure, approximately 440,000 reside on reservations. The higher numbers indicate a shift in identification as well as a rise in Indian fertility. "There were a lot of people who were ashamed of their Indian past, so they hid it," Cherokee sociologist Russell Thornton has explained. "But, a lot of people who went the assimilationist route have come back." Along with the overall Indian population, the number of federally recognized tribes is also rising. The Bureau of Indian Affairs listed 554 in 1995.

The current Indian agenda is to nourish this cultural pride and encourage the federal government to honor its promises to tribal peoples. "What's at stake," according to F. Browning Pipestem, an Indian attorney from Oklahoma, "is the ability of the tribes to develop as governments within the Indian country. The tribal government is the little voice that comes to our people that says, 'Hold on. Don't give up. Try another day.'" ◆

A Shoshone-Bannock woman and Yakima man display their traditional costumes during a powwow on the Fort Hall Reservation in Idaho. "There's self-respect at a powwow," declared one regular powwow participant, "tribal respect, national respect, respect for the powwow life, respect for being Indian."

RETURN OF THE BUFFALO NATION

When bison were hunted to near extinction in the 19th century, Indians lost more than the food, clothing, tools, and shelter the animal provided. They also suffered spiritually, for they regarded the buffalo as an irreplaceable gift from the Creator. Deprived of that gift and the power it conferred, people prayed for the return of the herds. Today, with the help of an organization called the InterTribal Bison Cooperative, those prayers are being answered.

The cooperative was conceived by Fred DuBray of the Cheyenne River Sioux, a Lakota tribe who maintained a small buffalo herd on their South Dakota reservation for subsistence and ceremony. Recognized by the federal government in 1992, the InterTribal Bison Cooperative has offered technical support to tribes with existing herds like the Cheyenne River Sioux and helped others such as the Pueblo peoples reintroduce bison to their homeland.

The organization has also sponsored educational programs to explain to groups around the country what the buffalo meant to Indians in the past and what it might mean for their future. As education coordinator for the cooperative, Carla Rae Brings Plenty of the Cheyenne River Sioux has spoken to audiences of all ages both on and off reservations, bringing with her a box filled with buffalo artifacts to illustrate how every part of the animal helped to support tribal communities. She and other members of the cooperative hope that native peoples will again make full use of this resource and celebrate the return of the Buffalo Nation—the mighty band of creatures that once dominated the grasslands and sustained the first Americans.

Bison graze below snow-clad peaks in Yellowstone National Park. The InterTribal Bison Cooperative has challenged the government policy of destroying buffalo that stray beyond the boundaries of Yellowstone as potential carriers of a disease harmful to cattle, proposing instead that strays be tested and the healthy animals shifted to tribal herds.

Hunters chase down buffalo in this colorful 1884 drawing by New Bear, a Gros Ventre whose people once pursued buffalo in the Yellowstone area. By the late 1800s, the herds had vanished and such hunts were evoked only in drawings and reminiscences.

RANGE OF BUFFALO

Scale of Miles
0   250   500

Although bison were especially important to Plains Indians, the animal once ranged from California to New Jersey and figured prominently in the lives of hundreds of tribes.

GIFTS FROM THE HERD

"The bison offered themselves to the people," writes elder Sidney Keith of the Cheyenne River Sioux. *"Every part of their body was useful."* Indeed, a typical bull weighing near-ly a ton (background) might yield 1,000 pounds of meat as well as a host of articles derived from its carcass, as sampled here, many of which had more than one function. The tail, for example, could serve as a fly swatter or as a whip for people scourging themselves in the sweat lodge. Tribes raising buffalo today continue to craft such articles for practical or ceremonial use.*

Carla Rae Brings Plenty of the InterTribal Bison Cooperative demonstrates one of the bison's innumerable applications to an eager group of schoolchildren by showing them an inflated buffalo bladder pouch, which could be used as a water vessel.

HORN USED AS DIPPER OR SPOON

PAINTING TOOLS MADE FROM HUMP BONE

BUFFALO-HIDE CONTAINER

HOOF-BONE TEETHING TOYS

HOOF SHEATH, TO BE BOILED DOWN INTO GLUE

DEFLATED BLADDER POUCH FOR STORING QUILLS

BUFFALO-TAIL FLY SWATTER OR WHIP

REVIVING A PRECIOUS RESOURCE

For Pueblo peoples living in the high desert country of New Mexico, just west of the Plains, the bison that once grazed in abundance nearby were an important asset. Early occupants of Taos Pueblo, nestled below the Sangre de Cristo Mountains, could pursue buffalo within sight of those peaks. The successful hunt was followed by a rite of thanksgiving that included dancing and feasting. By the 20th century, buffalo no longer roamed free in the area, but the people of Taos honored tradition by maintaining an enclosed herd. Since 1992, with the help of the InterTribal Bison Cooperative, they have increased both the size of the herd and its grazing area (background). Elsewhere in New Mexico, other groups have reintroduced bison to their land. In January 1995, Nambe Pueblo marked the arrival of a new herd—including some animals destined for the nearby pueblos of San Juan and San Ildefonso—with a celebratory Buffalo Dance.

At top left, men separate five buffalo for transportation from Nambe Pueblo to San Juan Pueblo in the spring of 1995. At bottom left, Joseph Martinez of San Juan Pueblo extends his hands in thanks for the animals to Herbert Yates, a holy man of the Winter Clan at Nambe. Handlers there sprinkled the departing animals with cornmeal and wished them farewell: "Take care, you are going to your final home."

Two male buffalo dancers at Tesuque Pueblo in 1925 (far left) and a female dancer appearing as Buffalo Woman in a ceremony there more than 50 years later (left) testify to the enduring importance of the bison to Pueblo culture. Traditionally celebrated in the winter, such dances were dedicated to the spirits that inhabited the animals and brought success to hunters.

ICONS
OF THE
PLAINS

The buffalo has long been central to the ceremonial life of Plains Indians, who still honor the strength and generosity of the animal through dances and prayers. Tribal lore celebrates the bison as a sacred link between the people and the powers watching over them. A legend of the Lakota says that the revered White Buffalo Calf Woman promised the people that bison would always be with them and left the Lakota a sacred pipe as a sign of that commitment. "It is a very sacred pipe and is to be treated as such," she said. "It connects you to all beings and to the Buffalo Nation." Today that pipe is cared for by Arvol Looking Horse, a spiritual leader from the Cheyenne River Sioux tribe. But Indians all across the Plains share in the belief that the bison is a sacred trust. From Choctaw country in Oklahoma to the Crow Reservation in Montana (background), the return of the buffalo signifies the renewal of ancient bonds between the people and their Creator.

A Crow woman and her daughter clean intestines removed from a freshly butchered buffalo (background, left). The Crow harvest a small number of buffalo from their herd each year for use in ceremonies and celebrations.

A Lakota buffalo effigy (top left), made from buffalo hide for display during the Sun Dance, and a buffalo skull hanging at the apex of a Crow Sun Dance lodge (bottom left) illustrate the spiritual importance of the creature to Plains Indians. Worshipers still perform the Sun Dance today, offering prayers and sacrifices to the supreme power who provides buffalo and other blessings.

HOMECOMING IN NEBRASKA

In 1994, for the first time in a century, buffalo roamed the Winnebago Reservation in Nebraska, where part of the tribe had relocated in the 1800s after being displaced from Wisconsin. For Winnebagos who welcomed the small herd of 11 animals to a 240-acre refuge on the reservation (background), the event marked the joyous reappearance of a creature that had nourished their ancestors and inspired the tribe's Buffalo Clan. Today, Winnebago elders use the herd to teach youngsters about their past and about the exemplary spirit of the animals. "The herd is just like a big family," explains keeper Louis LaRose. "They take care of each other."

A group of Winnebago preschoolers visit with the tribal herd (background). Other local schoolchildren have also made trips here to admire the bison and learn about their habits and history.

A hand-drawn card congratulating Louis LaRose on the birth of a new buffalo calf (below, right) reflects the excitement of the whole community over the addition to the herd.

Three Winnebago youths do their part to care for the growing herd by cutting weeds along the electric fence that guards the animals.

ACKNOWLEDGMENTS

The editors wish to thank the following individuals and institutions for their valuable assistance:

In the United States:

California: Covelo—Mike Lincoln, Round Valley Indian Reservation. Los Angeles—Chris Coleman, Museum of Natural History of Los Angeles County.

Connecticut: Mashantucket—Teresa Dzilenski, Mashantucket Pequot Museum and Research Center.

Nebraska: Winnebago—Louis LaRose, The Bison Project of the Winnebago Tribe of Nebraska.

New Mexico: Nambe Pueblo—Ben Yates, Nambe O-ween-ge; Taos Pueblo—Richard Archuleta, Office of Natural Resource Protection.

Oklahoma: Oklahoma City—Sherry Kast, United National Indian Tribal Youth, Inc.

South Dakota: Gettysburg—Fred DuBray, Cheyenne River Sioux Tribes, Crst Pte Hca Ka, Inc.; Rapid City—Carla Rae Brings Plenty, Mark Heckert, Inter-Tribal Bison Cooperative.

Virginia: Fairfax—Helen M. Scheirbeck.

Washington, D.C.:—Linda G. Hutchinson, National Indian Gaming Commission; Catherine Creek, Vyrtis Thomas, National Anthropological Archives, Smithsonian Institution.

Washington State: Seattle—Rebecca Andrews, Bill Holm, The Thomas Burke Memorial Washington State Museum; Bernie Whitebear, United Indians of All Tribes Foundation; Stan Shockey, University of Washington; Richard H. Engeman, University of Washington Libraries.

BIBLIOGRAPHY

BOOKS

Ambler, Marjane. *Breaking the Iron Bonds.* Lawrence: University Press of Kansas, 1990.

Benedek, Emily. *The Wind Won't Know Me.* New York: Alfred A. Knopf, 1992.

Berger, Thomas R. *Village Journey.* New York: Hill and Wang, 1985.

Bernstein, Alison R. *American Indians and World War II.* Norman: University of Oklahoma Press, 1991.

Blu, Karen I. *The Lumbee Problem.* Cambridge: Cambridge University Press, 1980.

Brodeur, Paul. *Restitution.* Boston: Northeastern University Press, 1985.

Brodie, Fawn M. *Richard Nixon.* New York: W. W. Norton, 1981.

Brophy, William A., et al., comps. *The Indian.* Norman: University of Oklahoma Press, 1966.

Burt, Larry W. *Tribalism in Crisis.* Albuquerque: University of New Mexico Press, 1982.

Cahn, Edgar S., ed. *Our Brother's Keeper.* Washington, D.C.: New Community Press, 1969.

Carnegie Foundation for the Advancement of Teaching. *Tribal Colleges.* Princeton, N.J.: Princeton University Press, 1989.

Champagne, Duane. *Native America.* Detroit: Visible Ink Press, 1994.

Churchill, Ward. *Struggle for the Land.* Monroe, Maine: Common Courage Press, 1993.

Coleman, James S. *Equality and Achievement in Education.* Boulder, Colo.: Westview Press, 1990.

Collier's:

1987 Year Book. New York: Macmillan Educational, 1987.

1988 Year Book. New York: Macmillan Educational, 1988.

1989 Year Book. New York: Macmillan Educational, 1989.

1990 International Year Book. New York: Macmillan Educational, 1990.

1992 International Year Book. New York: P. F. Collier, 1992.

1993 International Year Book. New York: P. F. Collier, 1993.

1994 International Year Book. New York: P. F. Collier, 1994.

Coltelli, Laura. *Winged Words.* Lincoln: University of Nebraska Press, 1990.

Cornell, Stephen. *The Return of the Native.* New York: Oxford University Press, 1988.

Culin, Stewart. *Games of the North American Indians.* New York: Dover Publications, 1975.

Danziger, Edmund Jefferson, Jr. *Survival and Regeneration.* Detroit: Wayne State University Press, 1991.

Deloria, Vine, Jr.:

Behind the Trail of Broken Treaties. New York: Delacorte Press, 1974.

Custer Died for Your Sins. New York: Macmillan, 1969.

God Is Red. New York: Grosset & Dunlap, 1973.

We Talk, You Listen. New York: Macmillan, 1970.

Deloria, Vine, Jr., and Clifford M. Lytle. *The Nations Within.* New York: Pantheon Books, 1984.

Dial, Adolph L., and David K. Eliades. *The Only Land I Know.* San Francisco: Indian Historian Press, 1975.

Doll, Don, S.J. *Vision Quest.* New York: Crown Publishers, 1994.

Dorris, Michael:

The Broken Cord. New York: Harper Perennial, 1989.

A Yellow Raft in Blue Water. New York: Warner Books, 1987.

Erdrich, Louise, and Michael Dorris. *Conversations with Louise Erdrich and Michael Dorris.* Ed. by Allan Chavkin and Nancy Feyl Chavkin. Jackson: University Press of Mississippi, 1994.

Ewing, Douglas C. *Pleasing the Spirits.* New York: Ghylen Press, 1982.

Fane, Diana, Ira Jacknis, and Lise M. Breen. *Objects of Myth and Memory.* Brooklyn: The Brooklyn Museum, 1991.

Fey, Harold E., and D'Arcy McNickle. *Indians and Other Americans.* New York: Harper & Brothers, 1959.

Fixico, Donald L. *Termination and Relocation.* Albuquerque: University of New Mexico Press, 1986.

Forbes, Jack D., ed. *The Indian in America's Past.* Englewood Cliffs, N.J.: Prentice-Hall, 1964.

Gordon-McCutchan, R. C. *The Taos Indians and the Battle for Blue Lake.* Sante Fe, N.Mex.: Red Crane Books, 1991.

Haas, Marilyn L. *The Seneca and Tuscarora Indians.* Metuchen, N.J.: Scarecrow Press, 1994.

Hertzberg, Hazel W. *The Search for an American Indian Identity.* Syracuse, N.Y.: Syracuse University Press, 1971.

Hirschfelder, Arlene, and Paulette Molin. *The Encyclopedia of Native American Religions.* New York: Facts On File, 1992.

Houlihan, Patrick T., and Betsy E. Houlihan. *Lummis in the Pueblos.* Flagstaff, Ariz.: Northland Press, 1986.

Hoxie, Frederick E. *The Crow.* New York: Chelsea House Publishers, 1989.

Hurtado, Albert L., and Peter Iverson, eds. *Major Problems in American Indian History.* Lexington, Mass.: D. C. Heath, 1994.

Indian Tribes as Sovereign Governments. Oakland: American Indian Lawyer Training Program, 1988.

Iverson, Peter. *The Navajos.* New York: Chelsea House Publishers, 1990.

Iverson, Peter, ed. *The Plains Indians of the Twentieth Century.* Norman: University of Oklahoma Press, 1985.

Johnson, Troy R., ed.:

Alcatraz. Los Angeles: Regents of the University of California, 1994.

You Are on Indian Land! Los Angeles: Regents of the University of California, 1995.

Jonaitis, Aldona. *From the Land of the Totem Poles.* New York: American Museum of Natural History, 1988.

Jonaitis, Aldona, ed. *Chiefly Feasts.* New York: American Museum of Natural History, 1991.

Josephy, Alvin M., Jr.:

Now That the Buffalo's Gone. Norman: University of Oklahoma Press, 1982.

Red Power. New York: American Heritage Press, 1971.

"Toward Freedom." In *American Indian Policy.* Indianapolis: Indiana Historical Society, 1971.

Katz, Jane B., ed. *This Song Remembers.* Boston: Houghton Mifflin, 1980.

Keegan, Marcia. *The Taos Pueblo and Its Sacred Blue Lake.* Sante Fe, N.Mex.: Clear Light Publishers, 1991.

Lawson, Michael L. *Dammed Indians.* Norman: University of Oklahoma Press, 1982.

Lazarus, Edward. *Black Hills, White Justice.* New York: HarperCollins Publishers, 1991.

Leacock, Eleanor Burke, and Nancy Oestreich Lurie, eds. *North American Indians.* New York: Random House, 1971.

Lesley, Craig, ed. *Talking Leaves.* New York: Dell Publishing, 1991.

Mankiller, Wilma, and Michael Wallis. *Mankiller.* New York: St. Martin's Press, 1993.

Maurer, Evan M. *Visions of the People.* Minneapolis: Minneapolis Institute of Arts, 1992.

McNickle, D'Arcy. *Native American Tribalism.* New York: Oxford University Press, 1973.

Meyer, Melissa L. *The White Earth Tragedy.* Lincoln: University of Nebraska Press, 1994.

Momaday, N. Scott. *House Made of Dawn.* New York: Harper & Row, 1968.

Nabokov, Peter, ed. *Native American Testimony.* New York: Penguin Group, 1991.

Nabokov, Peter, and Robert Easton. *Native American Architecture.* New York: Oxford University Press, 1989.

Native Americans and Energy Development II. Ed. by Joseph G. Jorgensen. Boston: Anthropology Resource Center, 1984.

Ortiz, Alfonso, ed. *Southwest.* Vol. 10 of *Handbook of North American Indians.* Washington, D.C.: Smithsonian Institution, 1983.

Paredes, J. Anthony, ed. *Indians of the Southeastern United States in the Late 20th Century.* Tuscaloosa: University of Alabama Press, 1992.

Parker, Dorothy R. *Singing an Indian Song.* Lincoln: University of Nebraska Press, 1992.

Parman, Donald L. *Indians and the American West in the Twentieth Century.* Bloomington: Indiana University Press, 1994.

Peroff, Nicholas C. *Menominee Drums.* Norman: University of Oklahoma Press, 1982.

Peterson, John M. *Aim on Target.* Lawrence, Kans.: Leonard Peltier Defence Committee, 1994.

Philp, Kenneth R. *John Collier's Crusade for Indian Reform, 1920-1954.* Tucson: University of Arizona Press, 1977.

Philp, Kenneth R., ed. *Indian Self-Rule.* Salt Lake City: Howe Brothers, 1986.

Prucha, Francis Paul. *The Great Father.* Vol. 2. Lincoln: University of Nebraska Press, 1984.

Rickard, Clinton. *Fighting Tuscarora.* Ed. by Barbara Graymont. Syracuse, N.Y.: Syracuse University Press, 1973.

Running, John. *Honor Dance.* Reno: University of Nevada Press, 1985.

Sandoval, Richard C., and Ree Sheck, eds. *Indians of New Mexico.* Santa Fe: New Mexico Magazine, 1990.

Sherman, Josepha. *Indian Tribes of North America.* New York: Portland House, 1990.

Silko, Leslie Marmon:
Almanac of the Dead. New York: Simon & Schuster, 1991.
Ceremony. New York: Penguin Books, 1977.

Snipp, C. Matthew. *American Indians.* New York: Russell Sage Foundation, 1989.

Stein, Wayne J. *Tribally Controlled Colleges.* New York: Peter Lang, 1992.

Steiner, Stan. *The New Indians.* New York: Harper & Row, 1968.

Swan, James A. *Sacred Places in Nature.* Sante Fe, N.Mex.: Bear, no date.

Swann, Brian, and Arnold Krupat, eds. *I Tell You Now.* Lincoln: University of Nebraska Press, 1987.

Szasz, Margaret. *Education and the American Indian.* Albuquerque: University of New Mexico Press, 1974.

Thomas, David Hurst, et al. *The Native Americans.* Ed. by Betty Ballantine and Ian Ballantine. Atlanta: Turner Publishing, 1993.

Trimble, Stephen. *The People.* Santa Fe, N.Mex.: School of American Research Press, 1993.

U.S. Bureau of Indian Affairs. *Indians in the War.* Chicago: U.S. Department of the Interior, Office of Indian Affairs, 1945.

U.S. Commission on Civil Rights. *Indian Tribes.*

Washington, D.C.: Government Printing Office, 1981.

U.S. Commission on Organization of the Executive Branch of the Government. *The Hoover Commission Report on Organization of the Executive Branch of the Government.* Westport, Conn.: Greenwood Press, 1970.

Viola, Herman J.:
After Columbus. Washington, D.C.: Smithsonian Institution, 1990.
Ben Nighthorse Campbell. New York: Orion Books, 1993.

Vizenor, Gerald:
The People Named the Chippewa. Minneapolis: University of Minnesota Press, 1984.
Wordarrows. Minneapolis: University of Minnesota Press, 1978.

Waddell, Jack O., and O. Michael Watson, eds. *The American Indian in Urban Society.* Boston: Little, Brown, 1971.

Wall, Steve. *Wisdom's Daughters.* Ed. by Harvey Arden. New York: HarperCollins Publishers, 1993.

Washburn, Wilcomb E., ed. *History of Indian-White Relations.* Vol. 4 of *Handbook of North American Indians.* Washington, D.C.: Smithsonian Institution, 1988.

Welch, James:
Fools Crow. New York: Penguin Books, 1987.
The Indian Lawyer. New York: W. W. Norton, 1990.

Whaley, Rick. *Walleye Warriors.* Philadelphia: New Society Publishers, 1994.

Wheeler, Richard. *Iwo.* New York: Lippincott & Crowell, 1980.

Wilkinson, Charles F. *American Indians, Time, and the Law.* New Haven, Conn.: Yale University Press, 1987.

Wise, Jennings C. *The Red Man in the New World Drama.* Ed. by Vine Deloria Jr. New York: Macmillan, 1971.

PERIODICALS

"Alcatraz Revisited." *American Indian Culture and Research Journal,* 1994, Vol. 18, no. 4.

Alvarez, Michelle. "Mount Shasta." *News from Native California,* Winter 1994/95.

American Indian Digest, 1994.

Baumgold, Julie. "Frank and the Fox Pack." *Esquire,* March 1994.

Blue Spruce, Duane. "Architecture As a Way of Life." *Akwe:kon Journal,* Fall-Winter, 1994.

Bodine, John J. "The Taos Blue Lake Ceremony." *American Indian Quarterly,* Spring 1988.

Boyd Gaming, July-August 1994.

Buckingham, Brooker. "Success Means Never Being Idle." *Calgary Herald,* January 27, 1995.

Campbell, Ben Nighthorse. "The Foxwoods Myth." *The New York Times,* March 29, 1995.

Churchill, Ward. "The Bloody Wake of Alcatraz." *American Indian Culture and Research Journal,* 1994, Vol. 18, no. 4.

Claiborne, William:
"Drained by Internecine War, Oglala Sioux Look to Past with Hope." *The Washington Post,* November 11, 1992.
"Rhode Island Stakes a Bet against the Narragansetts." *The Washington Post,* May 16, 1993.

Cloud Bringing Rain, and Marguerite Culp. "Our Blue Lake Lands." *Native Peoples,* Spring 1992.

Cornell, Stephen. "The New Indian Politics." *The Wilson Quarterly,* New Year's 1986.

Fisher, Marc. "The Voice of a People." *The Washington Post,* April 12, 1995.

Forrestal, Liz. "Indians Scouting for Better Land Deals." *Chemical Week,* June 28, 1978.

Franklin, Ben A. "Indians' Long Walk Winds Up in Capital." *The New York Times,* July 16, 1978.

Garvey, Megan. "The Great White Hope." *The Washington Post,* September 20, 1994.

Gilbert, Elizabeth. "Holy Cow." *Spin,* February 1995.

Haase, Eric:
"Repatriation." *The Lakota Times,* September 4, 1991.
"Homecoming with the Spirit Wind." *The Lakota Times,* September 4, 1991.

"Indian Gaming Is No Panacea for Indian Needs." *USA Today,* November 28, 1994.

"Indians Demand a Better Energy Deal." *Business Week,* December 19, 1977.

InterTribal Bison Cooperative 1993/1994 Annual Report, 1994.

Kenworthy, Tom:
"Hopis Feel Their Lifeblood Draining Away." *The Washington Post,* November 17, 1993.
"Idaho Indian Tribe Unveils Plans for National Lottery." *The Washington Post,* March 7, 1995.

Krakauer, Jon. "A Tribute to the Native American Spirit in Oregon." *Architectural Digest,* October 1993.

Layng, Anthony. "Sacred Sites." *Turtle Quarterly,* Spring-Summer 1993.

Lurie, Nancy Oestreich. "The Indian Claims Commission." *The Annals of the American Academy of Political and Social Science,* March 1978.

McAllister, Bill:
"At VA Hospital 'Medicine Man' Helps Indians Try to Beat an Old Nemesis." *The Washington Post,* June 9, 1991.
"Panel Calls for Legislation to Return Indian Remains." *The Washington Post,* March 1, 1990.

McCoy, Ron. "Navajo Code Talkers of World War II." *American West,* November-December 1981.

McGrory, Mary. "Ancient Winds Bring Fresh Air." *The Washington Post,* March 15, 1994.

Marcus, Ruth. "States Can Ban Peyote in Rites." *The Washington Post,* April 18, 1990.

Merida, Kevin. "For Campbell, Heritage Comes before Tradition." *The Washington Post,* September 20, 1993.

Mills, Jeanette C. "The Meares Island Controversy and Joe David." *American Indian Art Magazine,* Autumn 1989.

Native Peoples, Spring 1993.

Native Peoples, Winter 1995.

Northwest Indians Fisheries Commission News, Winter 1994.

"NWIFC Chairman Honored for Humanitarianism." *Northwest Indians Fisheries Commission News,* Summer 1992.

Passell, Peter. "Foxwoods, a Casino Success Story." *The New York Times,* August 8, 1994.

Pesce, Carolyn. "Crazy Horse." *USA Today,* July 19, 1990.

Pressley, Sue Anne. "Students Return to Language Roots in Oklahoma." *The Washington Post,* November 7, 1993.

Progress (Crazy Horse, S.Dak.), September 6, 1995.

"Return of the Natives." *The Hartford Courant,* May 22-29, 1994.

Ringle, Ken. "Casino on Sacred Ground." *The Washington Post,* February 15, 1992.

Sun Rhodes, Dennis. "My Home." *Native Peoples,* Spring 1993.

Taliman, Valerie. "The Heart of Everything That Is." *Turtle Quarterly,* Fall-Winter 1994.

Trescott, Jacqueline. "Tribe Donates $10 Million to Planned Indian Museum." *The Washington Post,* October 25, 1994.

Walsh, Edward. "Rise of Casino Gambling on Indian Land Sparks Controversy." *The Washington Post,* June 16, 1992.

Weinraub, Judith. "Museum Sets Policy on Indian Remains." *The Washington Post,* March 6, 1991.

Whitebear, Bernie. "Taking Back Fort Lawton." *Race, Poverty & the Environment,* Spring-Summer 1994.

"White Magic." *People,* October 3, 1994.

Wilson, Darryl. "Mis Misa." *News from Native California: California Indians and the Environment,* no. 1.

Yasui, Todd Allan. "Another Step for Indian Museum." *The Washington Post,* October 9, 1989.

OTHER SOURCES

Cowger, Thomas Wesley. "Sovereign Nations, Shared Identity, and Civil Rights." Unpublished thesis. Lafayette, Ind.: Purdue University, August 1994.

"Crazy Horse Memorial, Black Hills of South Dakota." Museum educational booklet. Crazy Horse, S.Dak.: Korczak's Heritage, 1990.

"Native American Rights Fund." Informational flyer. Boulder, Colo.: Native American Rights Fund.

"Native American Youth Leaders Gather in San Diego, June 15-19 to Develop 'Declaration of Unity.'" News release. Oklahoma City: United National Indian Tribal Youth, Inc., June 7, 1995.

"Speaking the Truth about Indian Gaming." Informational booklet. Washington, D.C.: National Indian Gaming Association, 1993.

"Unity among Nations." Declaration from the National UNITY Conference. San Diego: United National Indian Tribal Youth, Inc., June 15-19, 1995.

PICTURE CREDITS

The sources for the illustrations that appear in this book are listed below. Credits from left to right are separated by semicolons; from top to bottom they are separated by dashes.

Cover: Don Doll, S.J. **6-13:** © Eric Haase. **14:** Franklin D. Roosevelt Library, Hyde Park, New York. **17:** Department of Rare Books and Special Collections, Princeton University. **18:** UPI/Bettmann. **19:** Department of Rare Books and Special Collections, Princeton University. **21:** From *Information Respecting the History, Conditions and Prospects of the Indian Tribes of the U.S.,* Part V, by Henry R. Schoolcraft, Lippincott, 1855—photo by Alexander Gardner, courtesy Archives & Manuscripts Division of the Oklahoma Historical Society, neg. no. 1046.B; courtesy The Newberry Library, Chicago. **22:** AP/Wide World Photos—Tama Rothschild. **23:** Paul Abdoo—Peter Blakely. **24:** Marty Sohl. **25:** Denise Grant—photo by Greg Staats, courtesy Native Earth Performing Arts, Inc. **26:** "Apache Basket," artist unknown, A-106, photo by Larry Phillips, courtesy Institute of American Indian Arts Museum, Santa Fe, New Mexico. **27:** UPI/Bettmann. **28:** Terrance Moore. **29:** Sheldon Preston Photography. **30, 31:** National Congress of American Indians, Washington, D.C.—Harmon Griffin. **32, 33:** Courtesy Dennis L. Sanders (3), © Michael S. Crummett; courtesy Dennis L. Sanders. **35:** UPI/Bettmann. **36, 37:** National Archives, 75-N-REL-V3; Paul Natonobah, courtesy *The Photograph and the American Indian,* by Alfred L. Bush and Lee Clark Mitchell, Princeton University Press, 1994. **39:** Neg. no. 4495 (photo by George Hunt), courtesy Department of Library Services, American Museum of Natural History—KWA-Gulth Arts Ltd. **40:** Neg. no. 328734 (photo from Boas Collection), courtesy Department of Library Services, American Museum of Natural History—neg. no. 11604 (photo by Hastings), courtesy Department of Library Services, American Museum of Natural History. **41:** Richard Hunt, courtesy Sandra Hunt. **42:** AP/Wide World Photos. **43:** © 1995 Joel Grimes. **45:** Doug Martin/*Charlotte News.* **47:** AP/Wide World Photos. **48, 49:** Michael Collier; © Michael S. Crummett. **50:** © Michael S. Crummett. **52-55:** © Marcia Keegan. **56, 57:** Don Doll, S.J. **58, 59:** © David Muench. **60, 61:** Stephen Trimble (background), inset © Marc Muench. **62, 63:** Don Doll, S.J. (background), inset © Jeff and Alexa Henry, Roche Jaune Pictures, Inc. **64, 65:** © David Muench. **66, 67:** © Michael S. Crummett. **70:** Northwest Indian Fisheries Commission—from *As Long as the River Runs,* by Carol Burns. **71:** © Rex Rystedt Photography. **72:** Sherry Kast. **73:** Harmon Griffin. **74:** Harmon Griffin—© LeRoy DeJolie—Harmon Griffin. **75:** Harmon Griffin. **77:** Paul S. Conklin. **78:** © Stephen Trimble. **81:** Mary Kate Denny/Photo Edit. **82:** © 1995 Ed McCombs. **84, 85:** Photo by Fox Studios, Farmington, New Mexico, courtesy the Navajo Preparatory School, Inc. **86:** The Image Bank—UPI/Bettmann. **87:** AP/Wide World Photos. **88:** Golden Gate National Recreation Area, photo by Steve Danford and Tim Campbell, painting by Indian Joe Morris. **89:** *San Francisco Chronicle,* photo by Vince Maggiora. **90:** © 1970 Greg Gilbert/*The Seattle Times.* **91:** © 1995 George White Jr. **93:** UPI/Bettmann. **94:** © Bruce Fritz/*Capital Times.* **95:** © *Milwaukee Journal Sentinel.* **97:** Bob Fitch/Black Star. **98:** Photo by Don Ultang, Crazy Horse Memorial Archives—photo by Robb DeWall, Crazy Horse Memorial. **99:** Photo by Robb DeWall, Crazy Horse Memorial—© United States Postal Service, 1982. **100:** UPI/Bettmann. **101:** Steve Northup/Black Star. **102:** UPI/Bettmann. **103:** Michael Abramson/Black Star. **104:** Profiles West, Allen Russell, photographer. **105:** UPI/Bettmann. **106:** Mike Maple. **109:** Lois Flury, Flury and Company, Seattle—John Hughel, courtesy Statsney and Burke Architects. **110:** Montana Historical Society, Helena—Phil Bell, courtesy CTA Architects Engineers, Billings, Montana. **111:** Phil Bell, courtesy CTA Architects Engineers, Billings, Montana. **112:** Clifton Adams/National Geographic Image Collection—Gene Balzer Photography. **113:** Courtesy The Newberry Library, Chicago—Nick Wheeler, Wheeler Photographics, Inc. **114:** Neg. no. 336106 (photo by Dr. Frang), courtesy Department of Library Services, American Museum of Natural History—Shavey McManigal Architects; Chris Eden, courtesy Shavey McManigal Architects. **115:** Neg. no. 39991 (copy by Julius Kirschner), courtesy Department of Library Services, American Museum of Natural History—Ken Turner, courtesy Skidegate Band Council (2). **116:** Stephen Trimble. **118, 119:** © Masako Westcott; Robert C. Gildart. **120, 121:** Robert C. Gildart. **122, 123:** © Ted Wood. **125:** © Stephen Trimble—© Michael S. Crummett. **126, 127:** © 1979 Frank Johnston/Black Star. **128-131:** © Michael S. Crummett. **132, 133:** AP/Wide World Photos. **134:** © Michael S. Crummett. **137:** Barry Herem. **138:** © Eric Haase. **139:** Eric Haase, courtesy *Indian Country Today.* **141:** © Michael S. Crummett. **142:** J. R. Willis, courtesy Museum of New Mexico, neg. no. 98185. **143:** Richard Etchberger. **144:** Tony Bacewicz, *The Hartford Courant;* photo by Charles F. Lummis, Southwest Museum Collection, neg. no. N33550. **145:** Photo by Chris L. Moser, Riverside Municipal Museum, acc. no. A1-328—photo by Justin Kerr, courtesy The Brooklyn Museum, no. .05.588.7348. **146:** The Brooklyn Museum Archives, Culin Archival Collection, 6.3: Cushing Sketches—courtesy Dennis L. Sanders. **147:** Courtesy the Thomas Burke Memorial Washington State Museum, cat. no. 1988-117/15—Minnesota Historical Society, neg. no. E97.38/r4. **148, 149:** © Michael S. Crummett. **150:** Photo by Allen Phillips, courtesy Mashantucket Pequot Museum and Research Center. **151:** Allen Phillips (2)—artifact photos by Michael McAndrews, courtesy *The Hartford Courant* (3). **152:** Tebo Photography. **153:** Aaron Gooday-Ervin—photo by Tony Bacewicz, courtesy *The Hartford Courant.* **154, 155:** Photo by Tony Bacewicz, courtesy *The Hartford Courant;* Jock Pottle/Esto. **156:** © Michael S. Crummett. **157:** © Tom Kockle—Allen Russell, Profiles West, no. 942137. **158:** John Running. **160, 161:** Jeff and Alexa Henry, Roche Jaune Pictures, Inc. (background), inset Charles H. Barstow Collection, Eastern Montana College, photographed by Michael S. Crummett—map by Maryland CartoGraphics, Inc. **162, 163:** Jeff and Alexa Henry, Roche Jaune Pictures, Inc. (background), insets Eric Haase, courtesy InterTribal Bison Cooperative, Rapid City, South Dakota. **164, 165:** Richard Archuleta (background), insets (top) Jonathan Downey (2)—photo by Edward S. Curtis, courtesy Museum of New Mexico, neg. no.144657; John Running. **166, 167:** © Michael S. Crummett (background), insets © Michael S. Crummett; State Historical Society of North Dakota, no. 949—courtesy Dennis L. Sanders. **168, 169:** Louis La Rose, inset (top left) courtesy Louis La Rose.